MBTI Cheat Sheet

THE QUEST IN PODCAST

TABLE OF CONTENTS

1 **16 Psychological Types**
FUNCTION STRENGTHS AT A GLANCE

2 **2 x 2 x 2 Functions**
8 JUNGIAN COGNITIVE PROCESSES

3 **4 Dichotomies**
EXPLORING 8 LETTERS + UPDATED STATISTICS

4 **4 Temperaments**
GUARDIAN, ARTISAN, IDEALIST, & RATIONAL

5 **4 Quadras**
ALPHA, BETA, GAMMA, & DELTA

6 **8 Archetypes**
AN 8-FUNCTION MODEL BY JOHN BEEBE

7 **16 Intertype Relations**
FUNCTIONAL RELATIONSHIP BETWEEN 2 TYPES

8 **16 Types in Grip Stress**
TRIGGERS, FORMS, SOLUTIONS, & BENEFITS

i

PSYCHOLOGICAL TYPE

Personality type categorized by cognitive preferences

FUNCTION

A cognitive preference or mental process (like "a brain muscle")

DICHOTOMY

In psychological type: the contrasting categorization of introversion/extraversion, sensing/intuition, thinking/feeling, & J/P

TEMPERAMENT

A group of 4 types that have the same core values, needs, natural talents, & behaviors that are inborn preferences

QUADRA

A group of 4 types that are similar from sharing conscious functions

ARCHETYPE

In psychological type: a character role that embodies or represents how a function is experienced for a type

INTERTYPE RELATION

How two function stacks can cause attraction or repulsion

GRIP STRESS

A loss of conscious self-control due to unmanaged stress

TABLE OF CONTENTS

	A quick introduction	1
I	**16 PSYCHOLOGICAL TYPES**	**2**
	ISFJ Defender	3
	ESFJ Caregiver	4
	ISTJ Inspector	5
	ESTJ Supervisor	6
	ISFP Designer	7
	ESFP Entertainer	8
	ISTP Craftsman	9
	ESTP Explorer	10
	INFP Dreamer	11
	ENFP Inspirer	12
	INFJ Advocate	13
	ENFJ Mentor	14
	INTP Researcher	15
	ENTP Debater	16
	INTJ Mastermind	17
	ENTJ Commander	18

iii

II 2 x 2 x 2 FUNCTIONS   **19**

Introverted Intuition (Ni)   20

Extraverted Intuition (Ne)   21

Introverted Sensing (Si)   22

Extraverted Sensing (Se)   23

Introverted Feeling (Fi)   24

Extraverted Feeling (Fe)   25

Introverted Thinking (Ti)   26

Extraverted Thinking (Te)   27

III 4 DICHOTOMIES   **28**

Attitude: Introverted v. Extraverted (I/E)   29

Perceiving: Sensing v. Intuition (S/N)   30

Judging: Feeling v. Thinking (F/T)   31

1st Extraverted: Perceiving or Judging (P/J)   32

Updated MBTI Statistics (2018)   33

IV 4 TEMPERAMENTS   **35**

Guardian   36

Artisan   37

Idealist   38

Rational   39

V 4 QUADRAS — 40

- Alpha — 41
- Beta — 42
- Gamma — 43
- Delta — 44

VI 8 ARCHETYPES — 45

- 1st Hero — 46
- 2nd Parent — 47
- 3rd Child — 48
- 4th Anima/Animus — 49
- 5th Nemesis — 50
- 6th Critic — 51
- 7th Trickster — 52
- 8th Demon — 53

VII 16 INTERTYPE RELATIONS — 54

- Inner Quadra (Symmetric) — 55
- Outer Quadra (Symmetric) — 59
- Outer Quadra (Asymmetric) — 68

VIII 16 TYPES IN GRIP STRESS — 70

- Conclusion — 87
- Resources: **Quest In** — 88

A quick introduction

First off, **thank you so very much** for purchasing my **MBTI Cheat Sheet**!

I am so excited for you to use this **Ultimate 16 Personalities Visual Guide** to better understand the psychological types frameworks from the different angles!

This comprehensive visual guide was made so that you can **quickly reference** these pages for anything and everything foundationally essential when it comes to really understanding the 16 psychological types. I hope you enjoy it! This guide is jam-packed with some of the best frameworks developed in this typology. These frameworks excel at making the hidden aspects of personality visible to realize.

Lastly, I'm **Lizz**! Over 1/3 of my home library is personality books. I love psychology and personal development. These topics fuel my curiosity and love of learning. I love creating, almost as much as I love learning. My website **Quest In** is my creative outlet whenever my toddler is sleeping. Thank you for supporting us!

Copyright ©2024 by Quest In. All Rights Reserved.

Thank you for buying an authorized copy of this book. No part of this publication may be reproduced, stored, or transmitted in any form or by any means, electronic, mechanical, photocopying, recording, scanning, or otherwise without the prior written permission of the author. Requests to Quest In for permission should be addressed to contact@thequestinpodcast.com

SECTION ONE

16 PSYCHOLOGICAL TYPES
Functional strengths at a glance

1. **ISFJ** Defender
2. **ESFJ** Caregiver
3. **ISTJ** Inspector
4. **ESTJ** Supervisor
5. **ISFP** Designer
6. **ESFP** Entertainer
7. **ISTP** Craftsman
8. **ESTP** Explorer
9. **INFP** Dreamer
10. **ENFP** Inspirer
11. **INFJ** Advocate
12. **ENFJ** Mentor
13. **INTP** Researcher
14. **ENTP** Debater
15. **INTJ** Mastermind
16. **ENTJ** Commander

Note: The 4-letter code of a type is standard and official, but the following *character name* is rather an assigned unofficial nickname. *

2

ISFJ

STRENGTHS OF SI

- Hardworking, dutiful, reliable
- Stable & security-focused
- Excels with routine
- Strong reference to memories
- Detailed-oriented precision

STRENGTHS OF FE

- Empathic to the needs of others
- Naturally helpful & friendly
- Excels at harmonious relations
- People-oriented in values
- Ethical & considerate

POSSIBLE INTERESTS

- Communal gatherings
- Home & family life
- Traditional or conservative values
- Leisurely-paced hobbies

AT A GLANCE

- Attitude: **Introverted (I)**
- Primary Perceiving: **Sensing (S)**
- Primary Judging: **Feeling (F)**
- 1st Extraverted func.: **Judging (J)**
- Temperament: **Guardian**
- Quadra: **Alpha**

COGNITIVE FUNCTIONS

1. Si — INTROVERTED SENSING
2. Fe — EXTRAVERTED FEELING
3. Ti — INTROVERTED THINKING
4. Ne — EXTRAVERTED INTUITION
5. Se — EXTRAVERTED SENSING
6. Fi — INTROVERTED FEELING
7. Te — EXTRAVERTED THINKING
8. Ni — INTROVERTED INTUITION

ESFJ

STRENGTHS OF FE

- Empathic to the needs of others
- Naturally helpful & friendly
- Excels at harmonious relations
- People-oriented in values
- Ethical & considerate

STRENGTHS OF SI

- Hardworking, dutiful, reliable
- Stable & security-focused
- Excels with routine
- Strong reference to memories
- Detailed-oriented precision

POSSIBLE INTERESTS

- Socializing with friends frequently
- Experiencing life's traditions
- Learning new cultures
- Creating relations & bonds

AT A GLANCE

- Attitude: **Extraverted (E)**
- Primary Perceiving: **Sensing (S)**
- Primary Judging: **Feeling (F)**
- 1st Extraverted func.: **Judging (J)**
- Temperament: **Guardian**
- Quadra: **Alpha**

COGNITIVE FUNCTIONS

1. Fe — EXTRAVERTED FEELING
2. Si — INTROVERTED SENSING
3. Ne — EXTRAVERTED INTUITION
4. Ti — INTROVERTED THINKING
5. Fi — INTROVERTED FEELING
6. Se — EXTRAVERTED SENSING
7. Ni — INTROVERTED INTUITION
8. Te — EXTRAVERTED THINKING

ISTJ

STRENGTHS OF SI

- Hardworking, dutiful, reliable
- Stable & security-focused
- Excels with routine
- Strong reference to memories
- Detailed-oriented precision

STRENGTHS OF TE

- Efficient, effective, & useful
- Systematic organization
- Optimizing for costs/benefits
- Following guidelines & protocols
- Standardizing procedures

POSSIBLE INTERESTS

- Loved ones, home, & community
- Traditional or conservative values
- Leisurely-paced hobbies
- Optimized efficiency

AT A GLANCE

- Attitude: **Introverted (I)**
- Primary Perceiving: **Sensing (S)**
- Primary Judging: **Thinking (T)**
- 1st Extraverted func.: **Judging (J)**
- Temperament: **Guardian**
- Quadra: **Delta**

COGNITIVE FUNCTIONS

1. **Si** — INTROVERTED SENSING
2. **Te** — EXTRAVERTED THINKING
3. **Fi** — INTROVERTED FEELING
4. **Ne** — EXTRAVERTED INTUITION
5. **Se** — EXTRAVERTED SENSING
6. **Ti** — INTROVERTED THINKING
7. **Fe** — EXTRAVERTED FEELING
8. **Ni** — INTROVERTED INTUITION

ESTJ

STRENGTHS OF TE

- Efficient, effective, & useful
- Systematic organization
- Optimizing for costs/benefits
- Following guidelines & protocols
- Standardizing procedures

STRENGTHS OF SI

- Hardworking, dutiful, reliable
- Stable & security-focused
- Excels with routine
- Strong reference to memories
- Detailed-oriented precision

POSSIBLE INTERESTS

- Upholding traditions & culture
- Participating in a community
- Ensuring long-term security
- Managing others for optimization

AT A GLANCE

- Attitude: **Extraverted (E)**
- Primary Perceiving: **Sensing (S)**
- Primary Judging: **Thinking (T)**
- 1st Extraverted func.: **Judging (J)**
- Temperament: **Guardian**
- Quadra: **Delta**

COGNITIVE FUNCTIONS

1. Te — EXTRAVERTED THINKING
2. Si — INTROVERTED SENSING
3. Ne — EXTRAVERTED INTUITION
4. Fi — INTROVERTED FEELING
5. Ti — INTROVERTED THINKING
6. Se — EXTRAVERTED SENSING
7. Ni — INTROVERTED INTUITION
8. Fe — EXTRAVERTED FEELNG

6

ISFP

STRENGTHS OF FI

- Acknowledges own needs
- In touch with inner desires
- Honestly expressive
- Filters for authenticity
- Upholding personal standards

STRENGTHS OF SE

- Adaptive, quick responses
- Environmental awareness
- In touch with natural instincts
- Does well at a fast pace
- Creative aesthetically (art, style)

POSSIBLE INTERESTS

- Adventuring & exploring
- Creative artistic expression
- Designing a product to share
- Fashion, music, or trends

AT A GLANCE

- Attitude: **Introverted (I)**
- Primary Perceiving: **Sensing (S)**
- Primary Judging: **Feeling (F)**
- 1st Extraverted func.: **Perceiving (P)**
- Temperament: **Artisan**
- Quadra: **Gamma**

COGNITIVE FUNCTIONS

1. Fi — INTROVERTED FEELING
2. Se — EXTRAVERTED SENSING
3. Ni — INTROVERTED INTUITION
4. Te — EXTRAVERTED THINKING
5. Fe — EXTRAVERTED FEELING
6. Si — INTROVERTED SENSING
7. Ne — EXTRAVERTED INTUITION
8. Ti — INTROVERTED THINKING

ESFP

STRENGTHS OF SE

- Adaptive, quick responses
- Environmental awareness
- In touch with natural instincts
- Does well at a fast pace
- Creative aesthetically (art, style)

STRENGTHS OF FI

- Acknowledges own needs
- In touch with inner desires
- Honestly expressive
- Filters for authenticity
- Upholding personal standards

POSSIBLE INTERESTS

- Adventuring & exploring
- Performing or acting
- Hosting fun, engaging events
- Running an interactive business

AT A GLANCE

- Attitude: **Extraverted (E)**
- Primary Perceiving: **Sensing (S)**
- Primary Judging: **Feeling (F)**
- 1st Extraverted func.: **Perceiving (P)**
- Temperament: **Artisan**
- Quadra: **Gamma**

COGNITIVE FUNCTIONS

1. **Se** — EXTRAVERTED SENSING
2. **Fi** — INTROVERTED FEELING
3. **Te** — EXTRAVERTED THINKING
4. **Ni** — INTROVERTED INTUITION
5. **Si** — INTROVERTED SENSING
6. **Fe** — EXTRAVERTED FEELING
7. **Ti** — INTROVERTED THINKING
8. **Ne** — EXTRAVERTED INTUITION

ISTP

STRENGTHS OF TI

- Can explain logic step-by-step
- Analytical & strategic
- Intensely curious for knowledge
- Intrinsic motivation to learn *why*
- Understands frameworks & theories

STRENGTHS OF SE

- Adaptive, quick responses
- Creative aesthetically (art, style)
- Environmental awareness
- In touch with natural instincts
- Does well at a fast pace

POSSIBLE INTERESTS

- Adventuring & exploring
- Designing a product to share
- Crafting a beautiful creation
- Self-mastery & self-control

AT A GLANCE

- Attitude: **Introverted (I)**
- Primary Perceiving: **Sensing (S)**
- Primary Judging: **Thinking (T)**
- 1st Extraverted func.: **Perceiving (P)**
- Temperament: **Artisan**
- Quadra: **Beta**

COGNITIVE FUNCTIONS

1. Ti — INTROVERTED THINKING
2. Se — EXTRAVERTED SENSING
3. Ni — INTROVERTED INTUITION
4. Fe — EXTRAVERTED FEELING
5. Te — EXTRAVERTED THINKING
6. Si — INTROVERTED SENSING
7. Ne — EXTRAVERTED INTUITION
8. Fi — INTROVERTED FEELING

ESTP

STRENGTHS OF SE

- Adaptive, quick responses
- Environmental awareness
- In touch with natural instincts
- Does well at a fast pace
- Creative aesthetically (art, style)

STRENGTHS OF TI

- Can explain logic step-by-step
- Analytical & strategic
- Intensely curious for knowledge
- Intrinsic motivation to learn *why*
- Understands frameworks & theories

POSSIBLE INTERESTS

- Adventuring & exploring
- Competition in all forms
- Interacting with diverse people
- Running an interactive business

AT A GLANCE

- Attitude: **Extraverted (E)**
- Primary Perceiving: **Sensing (S)**
- Primary Judging: **Thinking (T)**
- 1st Extraverted func.: **Perceiving (P)**
- Temperament: **Artisan**
- Quadra: **Beta**

COGNITIVE FUNCTIONS

1. **Se** — EXTRAVERTED SENSING
2. **Ti** — INTROVERTED THINKING
3. **Fe** — EXTRAVERTED FEELING
4. **Ni** — INTROVERTED INTUITION
5. **Si** — INTROVERTED SENSING
6. **Te** — EXTRAVERTED THINKING
7. **Fi** — INTROVERTED FEELING
8. **Ne** — EXTRAVERTED INTUITION

10

INFP

STRENGTHS OF FI

- Acknowledges own needs
- In touch with inner desires
- Honestly expressive
- Filters for authenticity
- Upholding personal standards

STRENGTHS OF NE

- Creatively expansive with ideas
- Optimistic new perspectives
- Connects to related examples
- Exploration with an open mind
- Witty humor, cleverly engaging

POSSIBLE INTERESTS

- Astrology, mysticism, & healing
- Meaningful connections
- Personal growth & development
- Traditional philosophies

AT A GLANCE

- Attitude: **Introverted (I)**
- Primary Perceiving: **Intuition (N)**
- Primary Judging: **Feeling (F)**
- 1st Extraverted func.: **Perceiving (P)**
- Temperament: **Idealist**
- Quadra: **Delta**

COGNITIVE FUNCTIONS

1. Fi — INTROVERTED FEELING
2. Ne — EXTRAVERTED INTUITION
3. Si — INTROVERTED SENSING
4. Te — EXTRAVERTED THINKING
5. Fe — EXTRAVERTED FEELING
6. Ni — INTROVERTED INTUITION
7. Se — EXTRAVERTED SENSING
8. Ti — INTROVERTED THINKING

ENFP

STRENGTHS OF NE

- Creatively expansive with ideas
- Optimistic new perspectives
- Connects to related examples
- Exploration with an open mind
- Witty humor, cleverly engaging

STRENGTHS OF FI

- Acknowledges own needs
- In touch with inner desires
- Honestly expressive
- Filters for authenticity
- Upholding personal standards

POSSIBLE INTERESTS

- Aligned business endeavors
- Meaningful connections
- Personal growth & development
- Interpersonal interactions

AT A GLANCE

- Attitude: **Extraverted (E)**
- Primary Perceiving: **Intuition (N)**
- Primary Judging: **Feeling (F)**
- 1st Extraverted func.: **Perceiving (P)**
- Temperament: **Idealist**
- Quadra: **Delta**

COGNITIVE FUNCTIONS

1. Ne — EXTRAVERTED INTUITION
2. Fi — INTROVERTED FEELING
3. Te — EXTRAVERTED THINKING
4. Si — INTROVERTED SENSING
5. Ni — INTROVERTED INTUITION
6. Fe — EXTRAVERTED FEELING
7. Ti — INTROVERTED THINKING
8. Se — EXTRAVERTED SENSING

INFJ

STRENGTHS OF NI

- Long-term consideration
- Innovative problem-solving
- Strong future vision
- Trusts inner wisdom
- Awareness of repeating patterns

STRENGTHS OF FE

- Empathic to the needs of others
- Naturally helpful & friendly
- Excels at harmonious relations
- People-oriented in values
- Ethical & considerate

POSSIBLE INTERESTS

- Psychology & sciences
- Meaningful connections
- Personal growth & development
- Creating something for a cause

AT A GLANCE

- Attitude: **Introverted (I)**
- Primary Perceiving: **Intuition (N)**
- Primary Judging: **Feeling (F)**
- 1st Extraverted func.: **Judging (J)**
- Temperament: **Idealist**
- Quadra: **Beta**

COGNITIVE FUNCTIONS

1. **Ni** — INTROVERTED INTUITION
2. **Fe** — EXTRAVERTED FEELING
3. **Ti** — INTROVERTED THINKING
4. **Se** — EXTRAVERTED SENSING
5. **Ne** — EXTRAVERTED INTUITION
6. **Fi** — INTROVERTED FEELING
7. **Te** — EXTRAVERTED THINKING
8. **Si** — INTROVERTED SENSING

ENFJ

STRENGTHS OF FE

- Empathic to the needs of others
- Naturally helpful & friendly
- Excels at harmonious relations
- People-oriented in values
- Ethical & considerate

STRENGTHS OF NI

- Long-term consideration
- Innovative problem-solving
- Strong future vision
- Trusts inner wisdom
- Awareness of repeating patterns

POSSIBLE INTERESTS

- Communal engagement
- Meaningful connections
- Personal growth & development
- Teaching & mentorship

AT A GLANCE

- Attitude: **Extraverted (E)**
- Primary Perceiving: **Intuition (N)**
- Primary Judging: **Feeling (F)**
- 1st Extraverted func.: **Judging (J)**
- Temperament: **Idealist**
- Quadra: **Beta**

COGNITIVE FUNCTIONS

1. Fe — EXTRAVERTED FEELING
2. Ni — INTROVERTED INTUITION
3. Se — EXTRAVERTED SENSING
4. Ti — INTROVERTED THINKING
5. Fi — INTROVERTED FEELING
6. Ne — EXTRAVERTED INTUITION
7. Si — INTROVERTED SENSING
8. Te — EXTRAVERTED THINKING

INTP

COGNITIVE FUNCTIONS

STRENGTHS OF TI

- Can explain logic step-by-step
- Analytical & strategic
- Intensely curious for knowledge
- Intrinsic motivation to learn *why*
- Understands frameworks & theories

STRENGTHS OF NE

- Creatively expansive with ideas
- Optimistic new perspectives
- Connects to related examples
- Exploration with an open mind
- Witty humor, cleverly engaging

POSSIBLE INTERESTS

- Technology, sciences, computers
- Geopolitics, history, economics
- Cutting-edge research
- In-depth analysis & critiques

AT A GLANCE

- Attitude: **Introverted (I)**
- Primary Perceiving: **Intuition (N)**
- Primary Judging: **Thinking (T)**
- 1st Extraverted func.: **Perceiving (P)**
- Temperament: **Analyst**
- Quadra: **Alpha**

1. Ti — INTROVERTED THINKING
2. Ne — EXTRAVERTED INTUITION
3. Si — INTROVERTED SENSING
4. Fe — EXTRAVERTED FEELING
5. Te — EXTRAVERTED THINKING
6. Ni — INTROVERTED INTUITION
7. Se — EXTRAVERTED SENSING
8. Fi — INTROVERTED FEELING

ENTP

STRENGTHS OF NE

- Creatively expansive with ideas
- Optimistic new perspectives
- Connects to related examples
- Exploration with an open mind
- Witty humor, cleverly engaging

STRENGTHS OF TI

- Can explain logic step-by-step
- Analytical & strategic
- Intensely curious for knowledge
- Intrinsic motivation to learn *why*
- Understands frameworks & theories

POSSIBLE INTERESTS

- Technology, sciences, computers
- Geopolitics, history, economics
- In-depth analysis & critiques
- Engaged grounded discussions

AT A GLANCE

- Attitude: **Extraverted (E)**
- Primary Perceiving: **Intuition (N)**
- Primary Judging: **Thinking (T)**
- 1st Extraverted func.: **Perceiving (P)**
- Temperament: **Analyst**
- Quadra: **Alpha**

COGNITIVE FUNCTIONS

1. Ne — EXTRAVERTED INTUITION
2. Ti — INTROVERTED THINKING
3. Fe — EXTRAVERTED FEELING
4. Si — INTROVERTED SENSING
5. Ni — INTROVERTED INTUITION
6. Te — EXTRAVERTED THINKING
7. Fi — INTROVERTED FEELING
8. Se — EXTRAVERTED SENSING

INTJ

COGNITIVE FUNCTIONS

STRENGTHS OF NI

- Long-term consideration
- Innovative problem-solving
- Strong future vision
- Trusts inner wisdom
- Awareness of repeating patterns

STRENGTHS OF TE

- Efficient, effective, & useful
- Systematic organization
- Optimizing for costs/benefits
- Following guidelines & protocols
- Standardizing procedures

POSSIBLE INTERESTS

- Technology, sciences, computers
- Staying up-to-date to prepare
- Managing business at scale
- Seeking opportunities for success

AT A GLANCE

- Attitude: **Introverted (I)**
- Primary Perceiving: **Intuition (N)**
- Primary Judging: **Thinking (T)**
- 1st Extraverted func.: **Judging (J)**
- Temperament: **Analyst**
- Quadra: **Gamma**

1. Ni — INTROVERTED INTUITION
2. Te — EXTRAVERTED THINKING
3. Fi — INTROVERTED FEELING
4. Se — EXTRAVERTED SENSING
5. Ne — EXTRAVERTED INTUITION
6. Ti — INTROVERTED THINKING
7. Fe — EXTRAVERTED FEELING
8. Si — INTROVERTED SENSING

ENTJ

STRENGTHS OF TE

- Efficient, effective, & useful
- Systematic organization
- Optimizing for costs/benefit
- Following guidelines & protocol
- Standardizing procedures

STRENGTHS OF NI

- Long-term consideration
- Innovative problem-solving
- Strong future vision
- Trusts inner wisdom
- Awareness of repeating patterns

POSSIBLE INTERESTS

- Technology, sciences, computers
- Staying up-to-date to prepare
- Managing business at scale
- Seeking opportunities for success

AT A GLANCE

- Attitude: **Extraverted (E)**
- Primary Perceiving: **Intuition (N)**
- Primary Judging: **Thinking (T)**
- 1st Extraverted func.: **Judging (J)**
- Temperament: **Rational**
- Quadra: **Gamma**

COGNITIVE FUNCTIONS

1. Te — EXTRAVERTED THINKING
2. Ni — INTROVERTED INTUITION
3. Se — EXTRAVERTED SENSING
4. Fi — INTROVERTED FEELING
5. Ti — INTROVERTED THINKING
6. Ne — EXTRAVERTED INTUITION
7. Si — INTROVERTED SENSING
8. Fe — EXTRAVERTED FEELING

SECTION TWO

2 X 2 X 2 FUNCTIONS
Jungian cognitive processes

2 Types of Functtions	2 Processes for each Type	2 Attitudes for each Process
Perceiving	Intuition	 
	Sensing	 
Judging	Feeling	 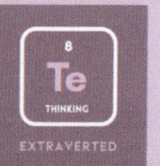
	Thinking	Ti INTROVERTED / Te EXTRAVERTED

INTROVERTED INTUITION

SUMMARY OF NI
- A **Perceiving** function: how we intake + process new information – *abstractly as concepts or ideas*
- An **Introverted** function: defined by *personal inner experience*

Examples of Activities that primarily use Ni:
- Meditating
- Planning long-term
- Novel problem-solving
- Identifying patterns & hidden meanings
- Abstractly exploring new perspectives
- Imagining new creative solutions
- Envisioning the future
- Realizing insights

Introverted Intuition excels at:
- Pattern recognition
- Future orientation
- Higher consciousness if pursued

Which types are Ni-Dominant:
1. **INFJ** Advocate (1st function Ni)
2. **INTJ** Mastermind (1st function Ni)
3. **ENFJ** Mentor (2nd function Ni)
4. **ENTJ** Commander (2nd function Ni)

How Ni-Se Interacts on an Axis:
- Extraverted sensing (Se) explores new real-world experiences
- Introverted intuition (Ni) takes sensory data from experiences to extract core principles

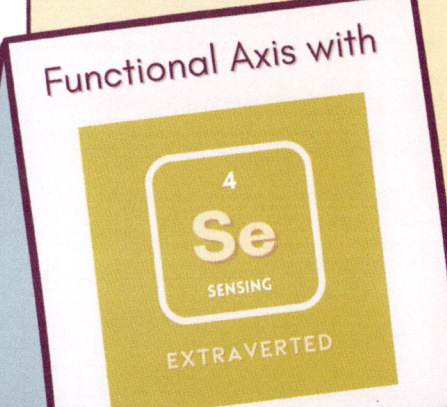

Functional Axis with

20

EXTRAVERTED INTUITION

SUMMARY OF NE

- A **Perceiving** function: how we intake + process new information – abstractly as concepts or ideas
- An **Extraverted** function: defined by outer external interactions

Examples of Activities that primarily use Ne:

- Identifying an emerging pattern
- Imagining possibilities
- Asking "What if..?"
- Finding discrepancies
- Linking a pattern to more examples
- Trying new ideas
- Brainstorming alternative outcomes
- Exploring dynamics

Extraverted Intuition excels at:

- Seeing many different potentials
- Quickly connecting a related topic
- Identifying hidden patterns

Which types are Ne-Dominant:

1. **ENFP** Inspirer (1st function Ne)
2. **ENTP** Debater (1st function Ne)
3. **INFP** Dreamer (2nd function Ne)
4. **INTP** Researcher (2nd function Ne)

How Ne-Si Interacts on an Axis:

- Introverted sensing (Si) has a strong memory of past experiences
- Extraverted intuition (Ne) uses past references to creatively imagine alternative new possibilities

Functional Axis with

INTROVERTED SENSING

SUMMARY OF SI

- A **Perceiving** function: how we intake + process new information – *concretely as facts & details*
- An **Introverted** function: defined by *personal inner experience*

Examples of Activities that primarily use Si:

- Telling or listening to personal stories
- Recognizing bodily sensations internally
- Optimizing comfort
- Routine repetition
- Recalling memories
- Learning history
- Focusing on safety & security
- Managing details

Introverted Sensing excels at:

- Detailed recollection of the past
- Securely stabilizing the present
- Upholding traditions & social norms

Which types are Si-Dominant:

1. **ISFJ** Defender (1st function Si)
2. **ISTJ** Inspector (1st function Si)
3. **ESFJ** Caregiver (2nd function Si)
4. **ESTJ** Supervisor (2nd function Si)

How Si-Ne Interacts on an Axis:

- Introverted sensing (Si) has a strong memory of past experiences
- Extraverted intuition (Ne) uses past references to creatively imagine alternative new possibilities

Functional Axis with

22

EXTRAVERTED SENSING

SUMMARY OF SE

- A **Perceiving** function: how we intake + process new information – concretely as facts & details
- An **Extraverted** function: defined by *outer external interactions*

Examples of Activities that primarily use Se:

- Exploring somewhere new & unfamiliar
- Competitive sports
- Quickly improvising to respond to a surprise
- Performing or acting
- Seizing a moment
- Noticing surroundings
- Creating art that is aesthetically pleasing
- Acting on instincts

Extraverted Sensing excels at:

- Attention to external sensory details
- Reacting in real-time with ease
- Aesthetic design of art or style

Which types are Se-Dominant:

1. **ESFP** Entertainer (1st function Se)
2. **ESTP** Explorer (1st function Se)
3. **ISFP** Designer (2nd function Se)
4. **ISTP** Craftsman (2nd function Se)

How Se-Ni Interacts on an Axis:

- Extraverted sensing (Se) explores new real-world experiences
- Introverted intuition (Ni) takes sensory data from experiences to extract core principles

Functional Axis with

INTROVERTED FEELING

SUMMARY OF FI

- A **Judging** function: how we make decisions + judgments – *valuing ethical considerations*
- An **Introverted** function: defined by *personal inner experience*

Examples of Activities that primarily use Fi:

- Journaling emotions
- Life choices reflection
- Aligned behaviors
- Identifying own core needs & values
- Analyzing the root of own & others' beliefs
- Accepting own natural motivations
- Prioritizing the self
- Speaking own truths

Introverted Feeling excels at:

- Accepting own personal experience
- Listening to determine compatibility
- Choices through alignment of beliefs

Which types are Fi-Dominant:

1. **ISFP** Designer (1st function Fi)
2. **INFP** Dreamer (1st function Fi)
3. **ESFP** Entertainer (2nd function Fi)
4. **ENFP** Inspirer (2nd function Fi)

How Fi-Te Interacts on an Axis:

- Introverted feeling (Fi) determines what's important to us personally.
- Extraverted thinking (Te) plans accordingly to accomplish what's important as a priority.

24

EXTRAVERTED FEELING

SUMMARY OF FE

- A **Judging** function: how we make decisions + judgments – *valuing ethical considerations*
- An **Extraverted** function: defined by *outer external interactions*

Examples of Activities that primarily use Fe:
- Helping someone else
- Giving a desired gift
- Accepting others as they are
- Genuine connections
- Relating through shared interests
- Interdependent relationships
- Offering support
- Role modeling

Extraverted Feeling excels at:
- Nurturing community & relationships
- Empathic listening & understanding
- Warm communication & attention

Which types are Fe-Dominant:
1. **ESFJ** Caregiver (1st function Fe)
2. **ENFJ** Mentor (1st function Fe)
3. **ISFJ** Defender (2nd function Fe)
4. **INFJ** Advocate (2nd function Fe)

How Fe-Ti Interacts on an Axis:
- Introverted thinking (Ti) creates personal frameworks of logic.
- Extraverted feeling (Fe) serves others best by using logical frameworks to choose appropriate behaviors.

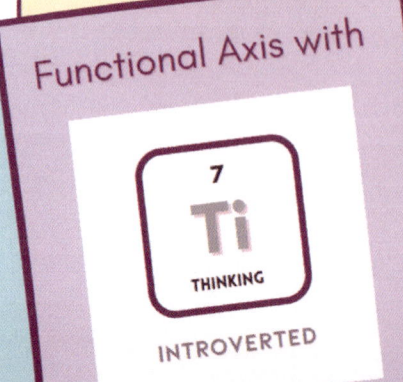

Functional Axis with

25

INTRODUCTED THINKING

SUMMARY OF TI

- A **Judging** function: how we make decisions + judgments – *valuing logical rationale*
- An **Introverted** function: defined by *personal inner experience*

Examples of Activities that primarily use Ti:

- Creating a framework
- In-depth analysis
- Researching
- Mathematical logic
- Becoming an expert of knowledge on a specific topic
- Effectively solving problems
- Explaining a principle
- Proposing a theory

Introverted Thinking excels at:

- Breaking concepts down into basics
- Critiquing, categorizing, & defining
- Explaining the *why* behind an idea

Which types are Ti-Dominant:

1. **ISTP** Craftsman (1st function Ti)
2. **INTP** Researcher (1st function Ti)
3. **ESTP** Explorer (2nd function Ti)
4. **ENTP** Debater (2nd function Ti)

How Ti-Fe Interacts on an Axis:

- Introverted thinking (Ti) creates personal frameworks of logic.
- Extraverted feeling (Fe) serves others best by using logical frameworks to choose appropriate behaviors.

Functional Axis with

EXTRAVERTED THINKING

SUMMARY OF TE
- A **Judging** function: how we make decisions + judgments – valuing logical rationale
- An **Extraverted** function: defined by outer external interactions

Examples of Activities that primarily use Te:
- Systematic planning
- Making a to-do list
- Assigning tasks to a scheduled time
- Organizing a space
- Making a visual depiction to explain
- Creating a standard or procedure
- Predicting outcomes
- Pros/cons analysis

Extraverted Thinking excels at:
- Organized efforts
- Efficient step-by-step execution
- Following guidelines for success

Which types are Te-Dominant:
1. **ESTJ** Supervisor (1st function Te)
2. **ENTJ** Commander (1st function Te)
3. **ISTJ** Inspector (2nd function Te)
4. **INTJ** Mastermind (2nd function Te)

How Te-Fi Interacts on an Axis:
- Introverted feeling (Fi) determines what's important to us personally.
- Extraverted thinking (Te) plans accordingly to accomplish what's important as a priority.

Functional Axis with

SECTION THREE

4 DICHOTOMIES
Exploring 8 letters + statistics

1. **I** - Introverted
2. **E** - Extraverted
3. **S** - Sensing
4. **N** - Intuition
5. **F** - Feeling
6. **T** - Thinking
7. **J** - Judging
8. **P** - Perceiving

MOST COMMON TYPES TO LEAST COMMON

1. **ISTJ**
2. **ISTP**
3. **ESTJ**
4. **ISFJ**
5. **ENFP**
6. **ISFP**
7. **INFP**
8. **ESTP**
9. **ESFP**
10. **ESFJ**
11. **INTP**
12. **ENTP**
13. **INTJ**
14. **INFJ**
15. **ENFJ**
16. **ENTJ**

Source: MBTI Manual for the Global Step I and Step II Assessments (2018)

See **1972-2002 MBTI Statistics** at: https://thequestinpodcast.com/mbti-statistics/

Comparison by ATTITUDES

INTROVERTS

The 8 types that lead with an **introverted 1st function** (Ni, Si, Fi, & Ti)

- Directed inwardly to the mind (internal experience)
- Slower pace of thinking
- Reflects before acting
- Enjoys improving on what's already in possession
- Fine without feedback from others to understand self
- Prioritizes doing less but with greater efficiency
- Defends against others' expectations
- Private, reserved, & self-aware of own needs

EXTRAVERTS

The 8 types that lead with an **extraverted 1st function** (Ne, Se, Fe, & Te)

- Directed outwardly to the world (external experience)
- Quicker pace of thinking
- Acts before reflecting
- Enjoys expanding to new possibilities
- Craves feedback from others to understand self
- Inclined to do more than what is necessary
- Influenced by others' expectations
- Outgoing, straightforward, & may not recognize own needs

Comparison by PERCEPTION

S | **N**

SENSORS

3 Si SENSING INTROVERTED | **4 Se** SENSING EXTRAVERTED

The 8 types with **introverted or extraverted sensing (Si or Se)** as their 1st or 2nd function

- Exact thinking: from the basis of observable facts
- Perception primarily by the senses (in the body)
- Intensely observant of the immediate environment
- Emphasis on usefulness
- Drawn to applied arts, such as crafts, dance, & sports
- Satisfied by pleasures & material security
- Relies on past experiences to solve problems
- Needs sensory evidence to believe something

INTUITIVES

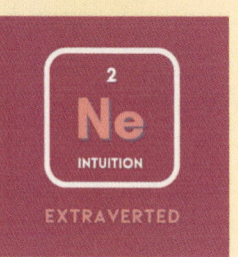

1 Ni INTUITION INTROVERTED | **2 Ne** INTUITION EXTRAVERTED

The 8 types with **introverted or extraverted intuition (Ni or Ne)** as their 1st or 2nd function

- Conceptual thinking: in the form of abstract ideas
- Perception primarily through thoughts (in the mind)
- Extremely active & vivid imagination
- Emphasis on unseen meaning
- Drawn to sciences, new discoveries, & innovation
- Inspired by future potential, such as the unknown
- Relies on creativity & ingenuity to solve problems
- Needs novel future possibilities to feel motivated

Comparison by JUDGMENT

T | **F**

THINKERS

7 Ti THINKING INTROVERTED
8 Te THINKING EXTRAVERTED

The 8 types with **introverted or extraverted thinking (Ti or Te)** as their 1st or 2nd function

- Prioritizes impersonal objective
- Decides impersonally with a basis of logic & efficiency
- Naturally independent in making decisions
- Generally uninterested in inner world of others & self
- Makes evaluations critically & with sober analysis
- Commitment to intellectual freedom & optimization
- Ability to prepare & plan for the future realistically
- Good sense of structure

FEELERS

5 Fi FEELING INTROVERTED
6 Fe FEELING EXTRAVERTED

The 8 types with **introverted or extraverted feeling (Fi or Fe)** as their 1st or 2nd function

- Prioritizes personal subjective
- Decides relationally with a basis of values & emotions
- Naturally considerate (of others) in making decisions
- Craves to understand the inner world of self & others
- Makes evaluations through ethics, such as "good/bad"
- Commitment to social responsibilities & empathy
- Ability to anticipate the needs & reactions of others
- Good sense of nonverbal communication

Comparison by
FIRST EXTRAVERTED FUNCTION
(DOMINANT OR AUXILIARY)

J | **P**

___ J

Fe FEELING EXTRAVERTED | **Te** THINKING EXTRAVERTED

The types with an **extraverted JUDGING function** as their 1st or 2nd function (Fe & Te)

- Goal: make a decision
- Prefers structure & planning
- Can be controlling & stubborn (but true to word)

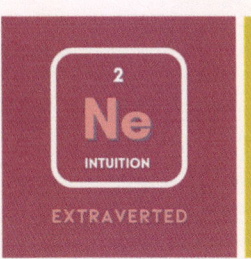

___ P

Ne INTUITION EXTRAVERTED | **Se** SENSING EXTRAVERTED

The types with **an extraverted PERCEIVING function** as their 1st or 2nd function (Ne & Se)

- Goal: find more information
- Resists committing
- Can be reckless & indecisive (but curiously adaptable)

IMPORTANT NOTE
"J" VERSUS "P" IS DIFFERENT FROM "JUDGER" VERSUS "PERCEIVER"

- "Judgers" & "Perceivers" are terms determined by a type's dominant function *(Is the 1st function a judging or perceiving function?)*
- Learn more on **Page 63**

UPDATED MBTI *Statistics*

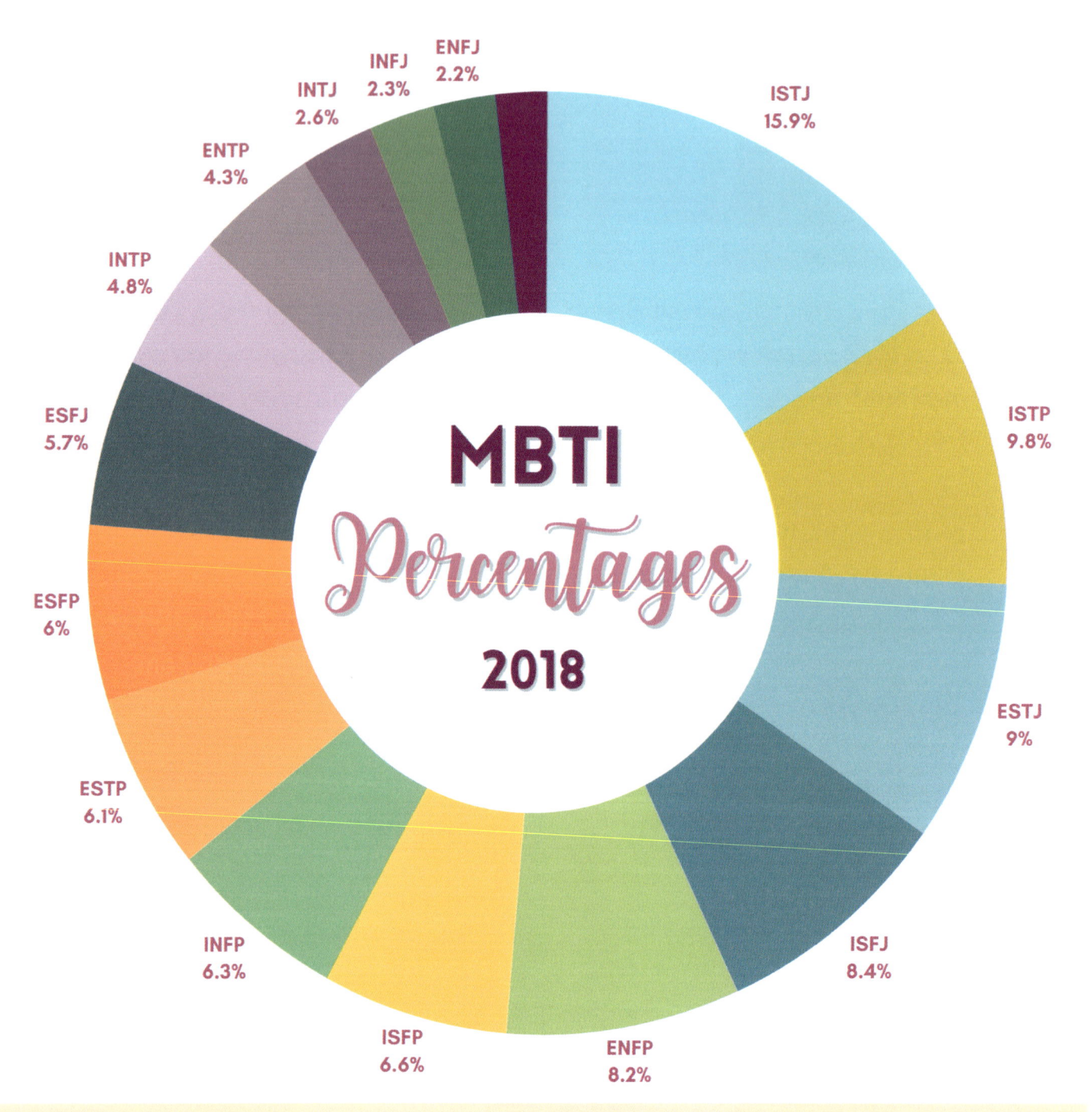

MBTI *Percentages* 2018

- ISTJ 15.9%
- ISTP 9.8%
- ESTJ 9%
- ISFJ 8.4%
- ENFP 8.2%
- ISFP 6.6%
- INFP 6.3%
- ESTP 6.1%
- ESFP 6%
- ESFJ 5.7%
- INTP 4.8%
- ENTP 4.3%
- INTJ 2.6%
- INFJ 2.3%
- ENFJ 2.2%

Source: MBTI Manual for the Global Step I and Step II Assessments Table 7.8

MBTI TEMPERAMENT DISTRIBUTION

Source: MBTI Manual for the Global Step I and Step II Assessments Table 7.8

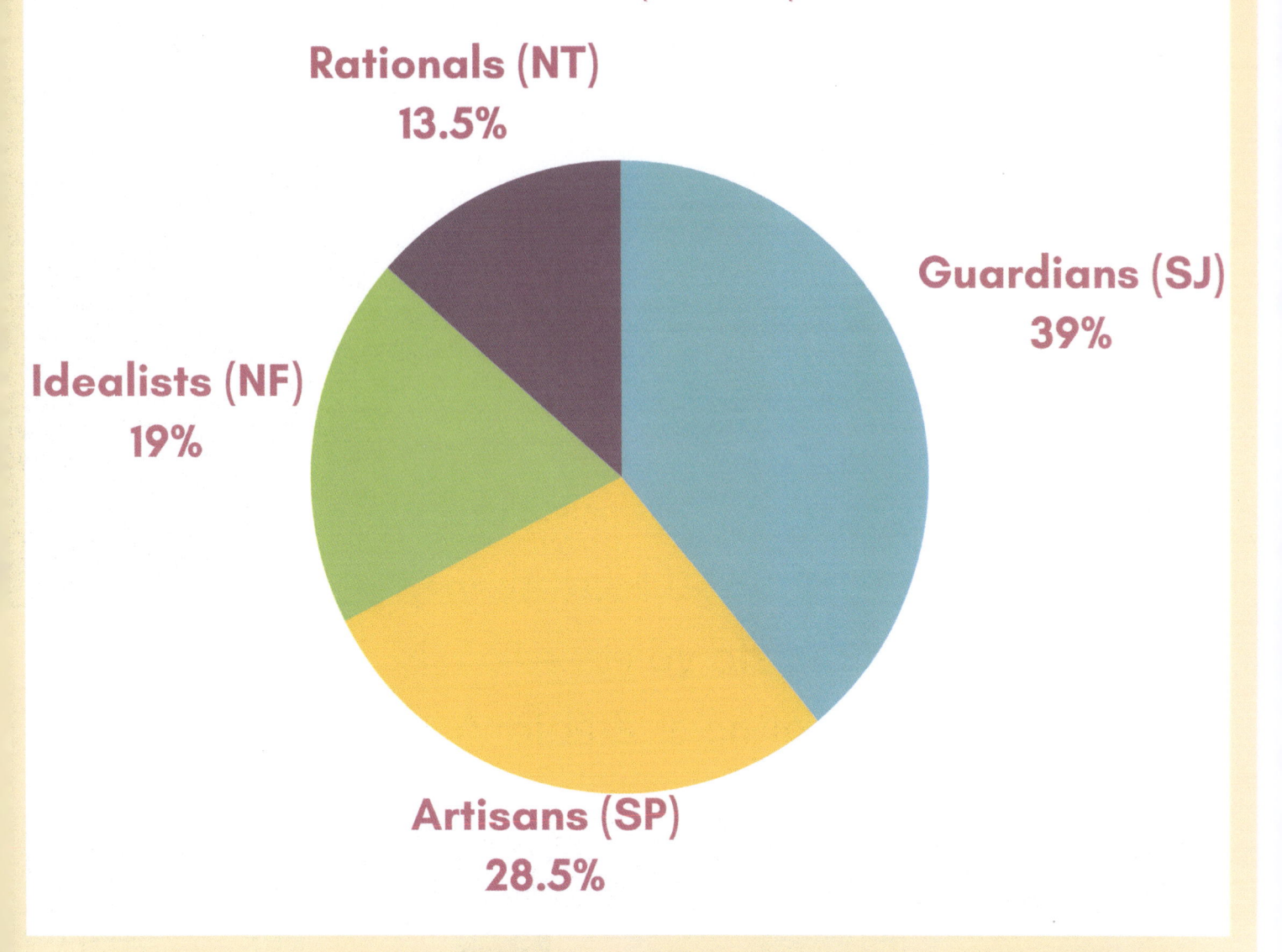

Rationals (NT) 13.5%

Guardians (SJ) 39%

Idealists (NF) 19%

Artisans (SP) 28.5%

MBTI DICHOTOMIES PERCENTAGES

Introverts 56.7% — I | E — **Extraverts** 43.3%

Sensors 67.5% — S | N — **Intuitives** 32.5%

Thinkers 54.3% — T | F — **Feelers** 45.7%

SECTION FOUR

4 TEMPERAMENTS

Guardian, artisan, idealist, & rational

35

GUARDIAN TEMPERAMENT

4 TYPES

SJ

1. **ISFJ** Defender
2. **ESFJ** Caregiver
3. **ISTJ** Inspector
4. **ESTJ** Supervisor

WORD CHOICE
Concrete (facts & details)

TOOL CHOICE
Cooperation (with others)

CORE NEEDS
Belonging, Stability, & Responsibility

VALUES
- Security & continuation
- Relationships & bonds
- Contributing to group
- Hierarchy & authority

FAVORITE ROLES
- Community organizer
- Logistical manager
- Traditionalist
- Stabilizer
- Support

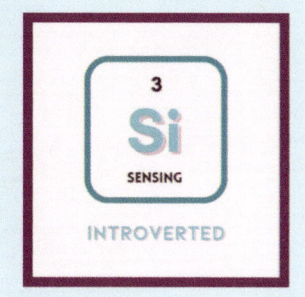

3 Si SENSING INTROVERTED

Natural Talents
- Logistics & measurement
- Protection & support
- Sequential thinking
- Attention to detail
- Rule enforcement

UNIQUE TO GUARDIANS
- Si-dominant with 1st or 2nd function **Introverted Sensing (Si)**
- Romantically **Attentive Teammate**
- Orientation to the **Past**
- Surprised when others deviate from authority or social structures

36

ARTISAN
TEMPERAMENT

4 TYPES

SP

1. **ISFP** Designer
2. **ESFP** Entertainer
3. **ISTP** Craftsman
4. **ESTP** Explorer

WORD CHOICE
Concrete (facts & details)

TOOL CHOICE
Utilitarian (effectiveness)

CORE NEEDS
Freedom, Impact, & Stimulation

VALUES
- Variety & spontaneity
- Pleasure & aesthetics
- Results from actions
- Devoted friendships

FAVORITE ROLES
- Persuader or Salesperson
- The *really fun* friend
- Negotiator
- Improvisor
- Executor

Se — 4 — SENSING EXTRAVERTED

Natural Talents
- Quick, adaptive reactions
- Tactical troubleshooting
- Seizing opportunities
- Colorful language
- Trusting instincts

UNIQUE TO ARTISANS
- Se-dominant with 1st or 2nd function **Extraverted Sensing (Se)**
- Romantically **Adventure Buddy**
- Orientation to the **Present**
- Thrives in fast-paced engagement, enjoying improvising & adapting

IDEALIST
TEMPERAMENT

NF

4 TYPES
1. **INFP** Dreamer
2. **ENFP** Inspirer
3. **INFJ** Advocate
4. **ENFJ** Mentor

WORD CHOICE
Abstract (ideas & concepts)

TOOL CHOICE
Cooperation (with others)

CORE NEEDS
Purpose, Meaning, & Significance

VALUES
- Empathic relationships
- Self-actualization
- Ethics & morality
- Authenticity

FAVORITE ROLES
- Catalyst or Transformer
- Harmonizer
- Counselor
- Mediator
- Foreseer

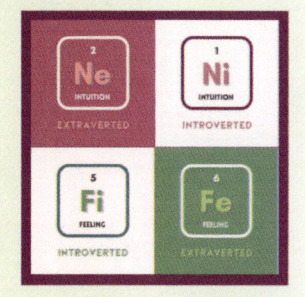

Natural Talents
- Imagining ideal possibilities
- Diplomatic interaction
- Personal development
- Relationship building
- Integrative thinking

UNIQUE TO IDEALISTS
- Top two functions are **Intuition and Feeling**, either **Ne & Fi** or **Ni & Fe**
- Romantically **Intimate Confidant**
- Orientation to the **Future**
- Relationship-centered & excels at unifying a diverse group for a cause

38

RATIONAL
TEMPERAMENT

4 TYPES

NT

1. **INTP** Researcher
2. **ENTP** Debater
3. **INTJ** Mastermind
4. **ENTJ** Commander

WORD CHOICE
Abstract (ideas & concepts)

TOOL CHOICE
Utilitarian (effectiveness)

CORE NEEDS
Competence, Mastery, & Knowledge

VALUES
- Improvement & progress
- Self-control & calmness
- Scientific principles
- Logical consistency

FAVORITE ROLES
- Engineer or Inventor
- Theorist or Visionary
- Systemizer
- Director
- Analyst

Natural Talents
- Preparing for the unexpected
- Differential reasoning
- Skepticism & critique
- Precise language
- Strategic design

UNIQUE TO RATIONALS
- Top two functions are **Intuition and Thinking**, either **Ne & Ti** or **Ni & Te**
- Romantically **Intellectual Companion**
- Orientation to the **Future**, but considers the past in analysis.
- Innovative problem-solvers that seek the most effective solutions possible

SECTION FIVE

4 QUADRAS
Alpha, beta, gamma & delta

δ **delta**

α *alpha*

gamma

beta

γ

β

the four QUADRAS

Quadras share a high degree of **internal comfort** within these groupings as they share all the same conscious functions. Each quadra has two temperamental energies the types embody.

40

Alpha QUADRA

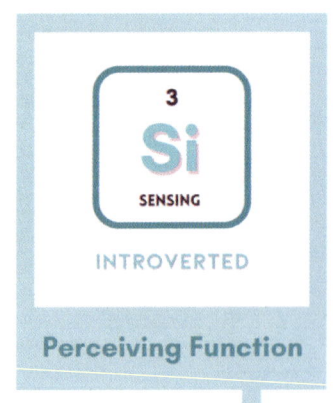

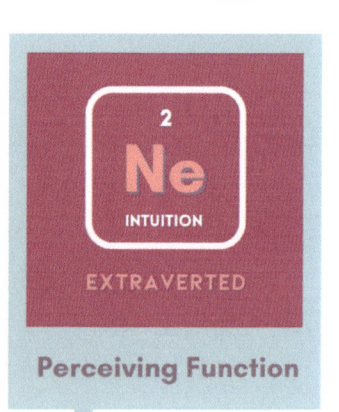

Si 3 SENSING INTROVERTED	Fe 6 FEELING EXTRAVERTED	Ti 7 THINKING INTROVERTED	Ne 2 INTUITION EXTRAVERTED
Perceiving Function	Judging Function	Judging Function	Perceiving Function

United by **family & research values**: full of friendliness & comfort, prioritizing loved ones

α

- Harmonious
- Hardworking
- Security-minded
- Low competitiveness

RATIONAL (1)

Partially Rational (1): Pure scientists that are driven by simple curiosity to understand the fundamental principles of everyday life

GUARDIAN

Partially Guardian: Caring contributors to their membership groups who welcome interdependent bonds

Beta QUADRA

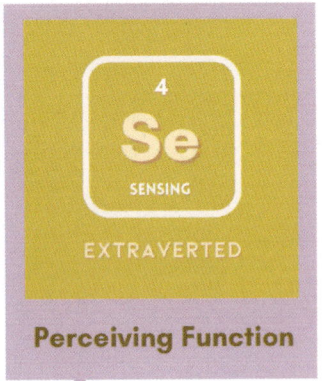

7 **Ti** THINKING INTROVERTED	4 **Se** SENSING EXTRAVERTED	1 **Ni** INTUITION INTROVERTED	6 **Fe** FEELING EXTRAVERTED
Judging Function	Perceiving Function	Perceiving Function	Judging Function

United by **romantic & strength values**: enjoying collectivism with an *"us versus them"* idealogy

β

- Easy conversationalist
- Competitive solidarity
- Charismatic
- Persuasive

IDEALIST

Partially Idealist: Social harmonizers who want to support the personal growth of people to contribute to a greater good for humanity

ARTISAN

Partially Artisan: Bold venturers who appreciate excitement & engaging activities, indulging in fun group atmospheres to form fraternal bonds

Gamma QUADRA

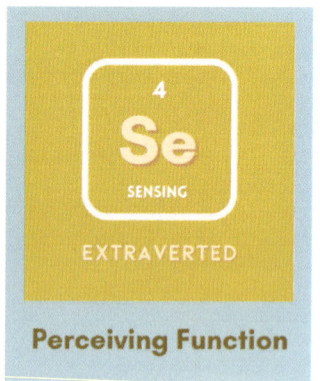

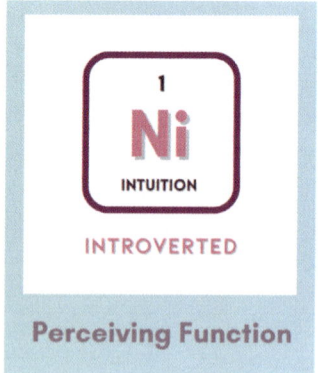

5 Fi FEELING INTROVERTED	4 Se SENSING EXTRAVERTED	1 Ni INTUITION INTROVERTED	8 Te THINKING EXTRAVERTED
Judging Function	Perceiving Function	Perceiving Function	Judging Function

United by **liberal & pragmatic values**: appreciating individual freedom of choice

γ
- Fiercely independent
- Shameless egoism
- Business-minded
- Desire to profit

RATIONAL (2)

Partially Rational (2): Benefit-driven optimizers who prioritize success, pragmatic relations, & innovation to maximize individual prosperity

ARTISAN

Partially Artisan: Bold venturers who appreciate excitement & engaging activities, indulging in fun group atmospheres to form fraternal bonds

Delta QUADRA

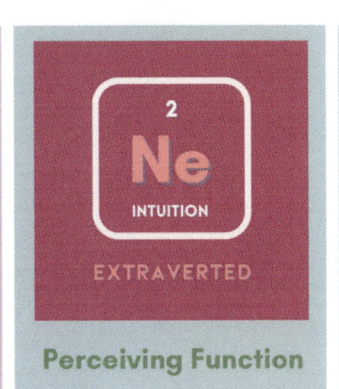

5 **Fi** FEELING INTROVERTED	2 **Ne** INTUITION EXTRAVERTED	3 **Si** SENSING INTROVERTED	8 **Te** THINKING EXTRAVERTED
Judging Function	Perceiving Function	Perceiving Function	Judging Function

United by **humanity & diligent values**: adhering to time-tested traditions & norms

δ

- Cooperative
- Stability-oriented
- Satisfied with what is already optimized

GUARDIAN

Partially Guardian: Caring contributors to their membership groups who welcome interdependent bonds

IDEALIST

Partially Idealist: Social harmonizers who want to support the personal growth of people to contribute to a greater good for humanity

SECTION SIX

8 ARCHETYPES

An 8-function model by Dr. John Beebe

Dr. John Beebe created an 8-function archetypal model that he developed through dream analysis. Each function is assigned **a character in our consciousness**, to illustrate how that function operates for each psychological type.

1. **Hero**
2. **Parent**   ⎫
3. **Child**   ⎬ CONSCIOUS
4. **Anima/Animus**   ⎭
5. **Opposite**
6. **Critic**   ⎫
7. **Trickster**   ⎬ UNCONSCIOUS
8. **Demon**   ⎭

1ST SUPERIOR OR DOMINANT FUNCTION

HERO
CONSCIOUS

Area of Focus: Strength & Pride

Operational Description:
- Organizes adaptation
- Initiates individuation

HERO (1ST) FUNCTION OF THE TYPES

Type	Function	Type	Function	Type	Function	Type	Function
ISFJ	Si (Introverted Sensing)	ISFP	Fi (Introverted Feeling)	INFP	Fi (Introverted Feeling)	INTP	Ti (Introverted Thinking)
ESFJ	Fe (Extraverted Feeling)	ESFP	Se (Extraverted Sensing)	ENFP	Ne (Extraverted Intuition)	ENTP	Ne (Extraverted Intuition)
ISTJ	Si (Introverted Sensing)	ISTP	Ti (Introverted Thinking)	INFJ	Ni (Introverted Intuition)	INTJ	Ni (Introverted Intuition)
ESTJ	Te (Extraverted Thinking)	ESTP	Se (Extraverted Sensing)	ENFJ	Fe (Extraverted Feeling)	ENTJ	Te (Extraverted Thinking)

2ND AUXILIARY FUNCTION
PARENT
CONSCIOUS

Area of Focus: Fostering & Protecting

Operational Description:
- Nurtures others
- Takes care of others

PARENT (2ND) FUNCTION OF THE TYPES

Type	Function	Type	Function	Type	Function	Type	Function
ISFJ	Fe (Extraverted Feeling)	ISFP	Se (Extraverted Sensing)	INFP	Ne (Extraverted Intuition)	INTP	Ne (Extraverted Intuition)
ESFJ	Si (Introverted Sensing)	ESFP	Fi (Introverted Feeling)	ENFP	Fi (Introverted Feeling)	ENTP	Ti (Introverted Thinking)
ISTJ	Te (Extraverted Thinking)	ISTP	Se (Extraverted Sensing)	INFJ	Fe (Extraverted Feeling)	INTJ	Te (Extraverted Thinking)
ESTJ	Si (Introverted Sensing)	ESTP	Ti (Introverted Thinking)	ENFJ	Ni (Introverted Intuition)	ENTJ	Ni (Introverted Intuition)

3RD TERTIARY FUNCTION
CHILD
CONSCIOUS

Area of Focus: Immaturity & Play

Operational Description:
- Innocent improvising to cope
- Vulnerable to occasional mistakes

CHILD (3RD) FUNCTION OF THE TYPES

ISFJ — Ti (7, Thinking, Introverted)	ISFP — Ni (1, Intuition, Introverted)	INFP — Si (3, Sensing, Introverted)	INTP — Si (3, Sensing, Introverted)
ESFJ — Ne (2, Intuition, Extraverted)	ESFP — Te (8, Thinking, Extraverted)	ENFP — Te (8, Thinking, Extraverted)	ENTP — Fe (4, Feeling, Extraverted)
ISTJ — Fi (5, Feeling, Introverted)	ISTP — Ni (1, Intuition, Introverted)	INFJ — Ti (7, Thinking, Introverted)	INTJ — Fi (5, Feeling, Introverted)
ESTJ — Ne (2, Intuition, Extraverted)	ESTP — Fe (6, Feeling, Extraverted)	ENFJ — Se (4, Sensing, Extraverted)	ENTJ — Se (4, Sensing, Extraverted)

4TH INFERIOR FUNCTION
ANIMA/ANIMUS
CONSCIOUS

Area of Focus: Embarrassment & Idealization (Insecurity + Aspiration)

Operational Description:
- Gateway to the unconscious

ASPIRATION (4TH) FUNCTION OF THE TYPES

Type	Function	Type	Function	Type	Function	Type	Function
ISFJ	Ne (2, Intuition, Extraverted)	ISFP	Te (8, Thinking, Extraverted)	INFP	Te (8, Thinking, Extraverted)	INTP	Fe (6, Feeling, Extraverted)
ESFJ	Ti (7, Thinking, Introverted)	ESFP	Ni (1, Intuition, Introverted)	ENFP	Si (3, Sensing, Introverted)	ENTP	Si (3, Sensing, Introverted)
ISTJ	Ne (2, Intuition, Extraverted)	ISTP	Fe (6, Feeling, Extraverted)	INFJ	Se (4, Sensing, Extraverted)	INTJ	Se (4, Sensing, Extraverted)
ESTJ	Fi (5, Feeling, Introverted)	ESTP	Ni (1, Intuition, Introverted)	ENFJ	Ti (7, Thinking, Introverted)	ENTJ	Fi (5, Feeling, Introverted)

Bedankt GTH!

5TH OPPOSING FUNCTION
NEMESIS
UNCONSCIOUS

Area of Focus: Frustration & Challenge

Operational Description:
- Defends by offending & seducing
- Avoids & is critical of the self

OPPOSITE (5TH) FUNCTION OF THE TYPES

Type	Function	Type	Function	Type	Function	Type	Function
ISFJ	Se (4) Extraverted	ISFP	Fe (6) Extraverted	INFP	Fe (6) Extraverted	INTP	Te (8) Extraverted
ESFJ	Fi (5) Introverted	ESFP	Si (3) Introverted	ENFP	Ni (1) Introverted	ENTP	Ni (1) Introverted
ISTJ	Se (4) Extraverted	ISTP	Te (8) Extraverted	INFJ	Ne (2) Extraverted	INTJ	Ne (2) Extraverted
ESTJ	Ti (7) Introverted	ESTP	Si (3) Introverted	ENFJ	Fi (5) Introverted	ENTJ	Ti (7) Introverted

50

6TH SENEX/WITCH FUNCTION
CRITIC
UNCONSCIOUS

Area of Focus: Limit-setting & Control

Operational Description:
- Defends by refusing & belittling
- Sets limits to deactivate

CRITICAL (6TH) FUNCTION OF THE TYPES

Type	Function	Type	Function	Type	Function	Type	Function
ISFJ	Fi (Introverted Feeling)	ISFP	Si (Introverted Sensing)	INFP	Ni (Introverted Intuition)	INTP	Ni (Introverted Intuition)
ESFJ	Se (Extraverted Sensing)	ESFP	Fe (Extraverted Feeling)	ENFP	Fe (Extraverted Feeling)	ENTP	Te (Extraverted Thinking)
ISTJ	Ti (Introverted Thinking)	ISTP	Si (Introverted Sensing)	INFJ	Fi (Introverted Feeling)	INTJ	Ti (Introverted Thinking)
ESTJ	Se (Extraverted Sensing)	ESTP	Te (Extraverted Thinking)	ENFJ	Ne (Extraverted Intuition)	ENTJ	Ne (Extraverted Intuition)

7TH BLINDSPOT FUNCTION
TRICKSTER
UNCONSCIOUS

Area of Focus: Manipulation & Paradox

Operational Description:
- Mischievously underdeveloped
- Disrespects rules & boundaries

BLINDSPOT (7TH) FUNCTION OF THE TYPES

Type	Function	Type	Function	Type	Function	Type	Function
ISFJ	Te (Extraverted Thinking)	ISFP	Ne (Extraverted Intuition)	INFP	Se (Extraverted Sensing)	INTP	Se (Extraverted Sensing)
ESFJ	Ni (Introverted Intuition)	ESFP	Ti (Introverted Thinking)	ENFP	Ti (Introverted Thinking)	ENTP	Fi (Introverted Feeling)
ISTJ	Fe (Extraverted Feeling)	ISTP	Ne (Extraverted Intuition)	INFJ	Te (Extraverted Thinking)	INTJ	Fe (Extraverted Feeling)
ESTJ	Ni (Introverted Intuition)	ESTP	Fi (Introverted Feeling)	ENFJ	Si (Introverted Sensing)	ENTJ	Si (Introverted Sensing)

8TH TRIGGER FUNCTION
DEMON
UNCONSCIOUS

Area of Focus: Undermining Self + Others, yet Opportunity for Redemption

Operational Description:
- Feels most foreignly "Other" to us

TRIGGER (8TH) FUNCTION OF THE TYPES

Type	Function	Type	Function	Type	Function	Type	Function
ISFJ	Ni (Introverted Intuition)	ISFP	Ti (Introverted Thinking)	INFP	Ti (Introverted Thinking)	INTP	Fi (Introverted Feeling)
ESFJ	Te (Extraverted Thinking)	ESFP	Ne (Extraverted Intuition)	ENFP	Se (Extraverted Sensing)	ENTP	Se (Extraverted Sensing)
ISTJ	Ni (Introverted Intuition)	ISTP	Fi (Introverted Feeling)	INFJ	Si (Introverted Sensing)	INTJ	Si (Introverted Sensing)
ESTJ	Fe (Extraverted Feeling)	ESTP	Ne (Extraverted Intuition)	ENFJ	Te (Extraverted Thinking)	ENTJ	Fe (Extraverted Feeling)

SECTION SEVEN

16 INTERTYPE RELATIONS

Functional relationship between 2 Types

INNER QUADRA RELATIONS

a. **Identity (1)**
b. **Mirror (2)**
c. **Activity (3)**
d. **Duality (4)**

OUTER QUADRA RELATIONS

a. No shared functions
   i. **Quasi-Identical (5)**
   ii. **Extinguishing (6)**
   iii. **Super-Ego (7)**
   iv. **Conflict (8)**

b. Partially shared functions
   i. **Half-Duality (9)**
   ii. **Kindred (10)**
   iii. **Mirage (11)**
   iv. **Look-a-like (12)**
   v. **Supervisor (13)**
   vi. **Supervisee (14)**
   vii. **Benefactor (15)**
   viii. **Beneficiary (16)**

IMPORTANT NOTE

The Quadras (section 4) + this section *Intertype Relations* are frameworks developed from **Socionics** - which is **different but parallel to MBTI**. Socionics concepts are quite *advanced* but offer great contributions to understanding predictable interactions between types based on functional compatibilities.

INNER QUADRA SYMMETRIC

IDENTITY

NOTES
- Possible attraction
- Easy compatibility
- Type same as own
- Helps to better understand the self
- Mutual recognition of intent in actions

Types **share ALL** their *conscious* functions: natural comfort & easy communication

SAME SAME SAME SAME

INFJ — INFJ

1 ↔ 1
2 ↔ 2
3 ↔ 3
4 ↔ 4
5　　5
6　　6
7　　7
8　　8

1

INFJ — INFJ	INTJ — INTJ	ISTJ — ISTJ	ESFP — ESFP
INFP — INFP	INTP — INTP	ISFJ — ISFJ	ISFP — ISFP
ENFJ — ENFJ	ENTP — ENTP	ESFJ — ESFJ	ISTP — ISTP
ENFP — ENFP	ENTJ — ENTJ	ESTJ — ESTJ	ESTP — ESTP

55

INNER QUADRA SYMMETRIC

MIRROR

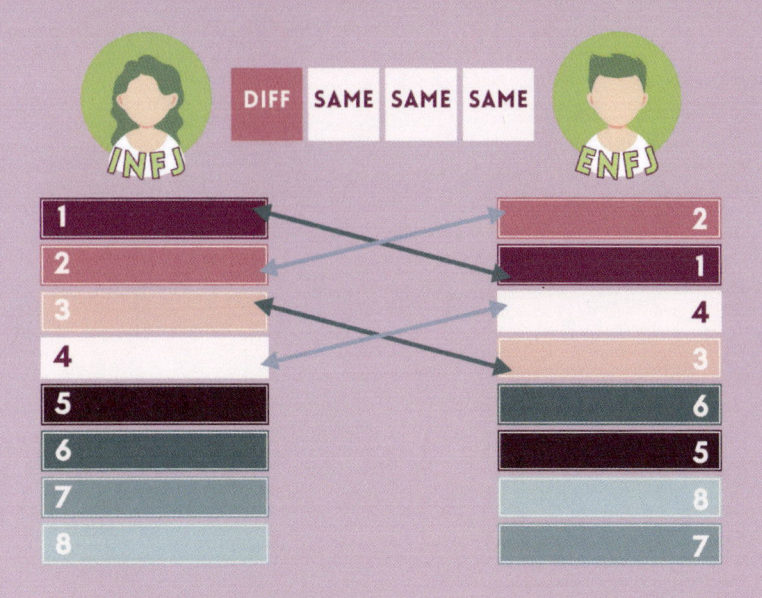

NOTES
- Medium attraction
- Easy compatibility
- Contrast **1st** letter
- *Dominant* function is other's *Auxiliary*
- Appreciate's the other's strengths

Types **share ALL** their *conscious* functions: natural comfort & easy communication

INFJ — ENFJ

DIFF | SAME | SAME | SAME

INFJ	ENFJ
1	2
2	1
3	4
4	3
5	6
6	5
7	8
8	7

1 2

- INFJ — ENFJ
- INTJ — ENTJ
- ESFP — ISFP
- ISFJ — ESFJ
- ENTP — INTP
- ENFP — INFP
- ESTJ — ISTJ
- ESTP — ISTP

56

INNER QUADRA SYMMETRIC

ACTIVITY

NOTES
- Easy attraction
- Easy compatibility
- Contrast **3** letters
- *Dominant* function is other's *Teritiary*
- Comfortable, yet a bit distant

Types **share ALL** their *conscious* functions: natural comfort & easy communication

INFJ — SAME | DIFF | DIFF | DIFF — ISTP

INFJ	ISTP
1	3
2	4
3	1
4	2
5	7
6	8
7	5
8	6

1 2 **3**

INFJ ISTP

ISTJ INFP

INTP ISFJ

ISFP INTJ

ESFJ ENTP

ENFP ESTJ

ENTJ ESFP

ESTP ENFS

57

INNERQUADRA SYMMETRIC

DUALITY

NOTES
- Easy attraction
- Easy compatibility
- Contrast **all** letters
- *Dominant* function is other's *Inferior*
- Reflection of type's conscious top 4

Types **share ALL** their *conscious* functions: natural comfort & easy communication

INFJ — DIFF DIFF DIFF DIFF — ESTP

1 2 3 4 5 6 7 8 ↔ 4 3 2 1 8 7 6 5

1 2 3 **4**

INFP — ESTJ
ENFJ — ISTP
ENTJ — ISFP
ISTJ — ENFP
ISFJ — ENTP
ESFJ — INTP
ESFP — INTJ
ESTP — INFJ

58

QUASI-IDENTICAL

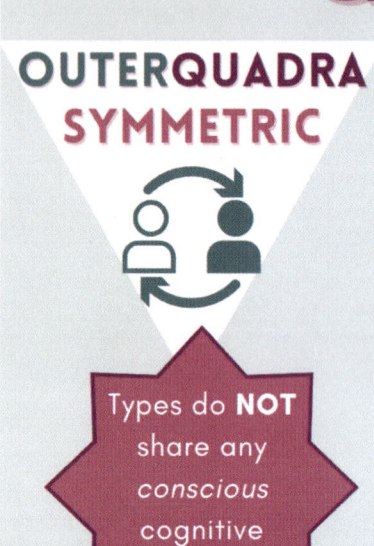

OUTERQUADRA SYMMETRIC

Types do **NOT** share any *conscious* cognitive functions

	SAME	SAME	SAME	DIFF	
INFJ					INFP

INFJ:
1
2
3
4
5
6
7
8

INFP:
6
5
8
7
2
1
4
3

NOTES
- Some attraction
- Easy compatibility
- Potential repulsion
- Contrast **last** letter
- Reflection of shadow functions in different order

1 2 3 4 **5**

INFJ – INFP

INTP – INTJ

ENTP – ENTJ

ENFP – ENFJ

ISTJ – ISTP

ISFJ – ISFP

ESFJ – ESFP

ESTJ – ESTP

59

EXTINGUISHING

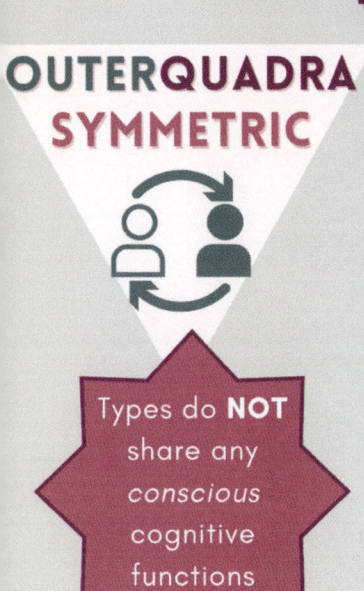

OUTERQUADRA SYMMETRIC

Types do **NOT** share any *conscious* cognitive functions

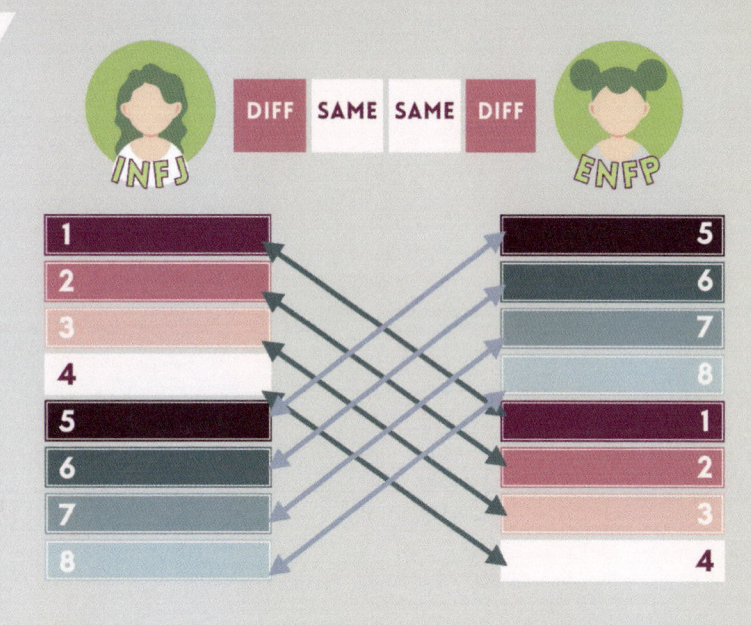

INFJ — DIFF SAME SAME DIFF — ENFP

NOTES
- Medium attraction
- Easy compatibility
- Possible repulsion
- Contrast **1st & 4th** letters
- Reflection of type's shadow functions

1 2 3 4 5 **6**

INFJ ENFP

ISTJ ESTP

ESFP ISFJ

INTP ENTJ

ENFJ INFP

ESFJ ISFP

ISTP ESTJ

ENTP INTJ

SUPER-EGO

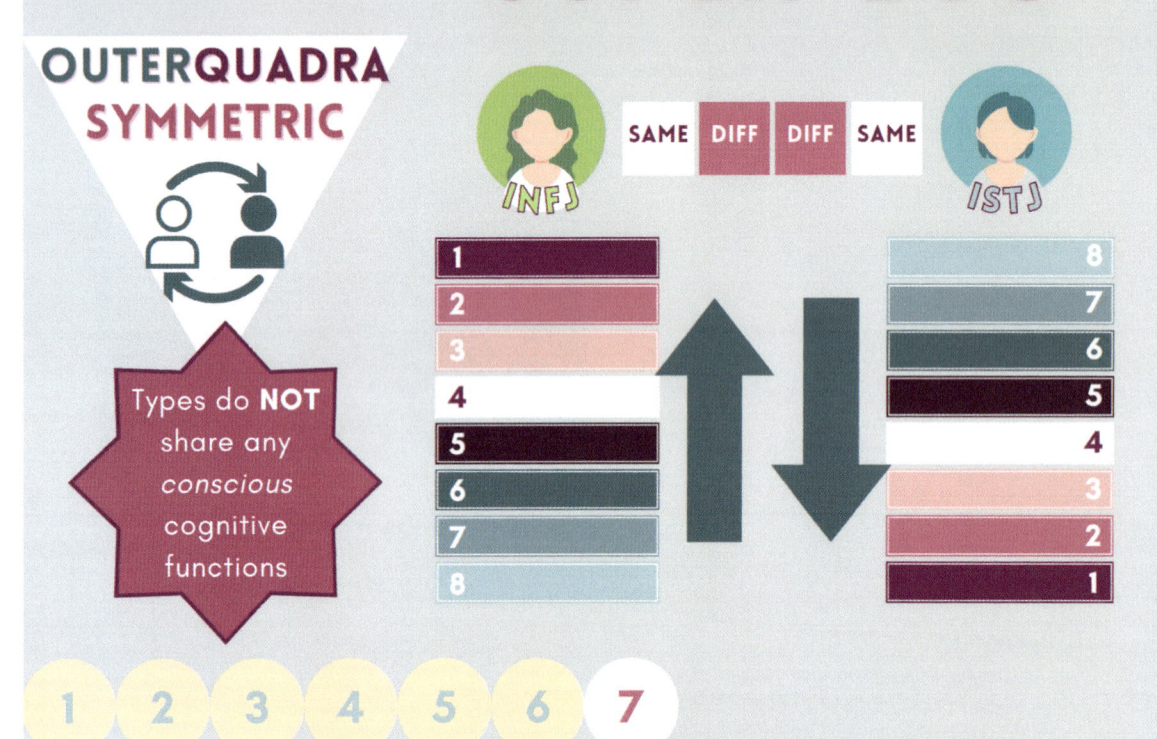

OUTERQUADRA SYMMETRIC

Types do **NOT** share any *conscious* cognitive functions

INFJ — SAME | DIFF | DIFF | SAME — ISTJ

INFJ	ISTJ
1	8
2	7
3	6
4	5
5	4
6	3
7	2
8	1

NOTES
- Possible medium compatibility
- Easy repulsion
- Contrast **2nd & 3rd** letters
- *Dominant* function is other's *Trigger*

1 2 3 4 5 6 **7**

INFJ — ISTJ

INTP — ISFP   ISFJ — INTJ

ENFJ — ESTJ   ENTP — ESFP   ESFJ — ENTJ   ISTP — INFP

ESTP — ENFP

61

CONFLICT

OUTERQUADRA SYMMETRIC

Types do **NOT** share any *conscious* cognitive functions

INFJ — DIFF DIFF DIFF SAME — ESTJ

NOTES
- Very easy repulsion
- Contrast **3** letter
- *Dominant* function is other's *Blindspot*
- **TIP:** Shorten length of time spent alone together

1 2 3 4 5 6 7 **8**

INFJ ESTJ

INTP ESFP

ISFJ ENTJ

ENFJ ISTJ

ENTP ISFP

ESFJ INTJ

ISTP ENFP

ESTP INFP

62

"JUDGER" VERSUS "PERCEIVER"

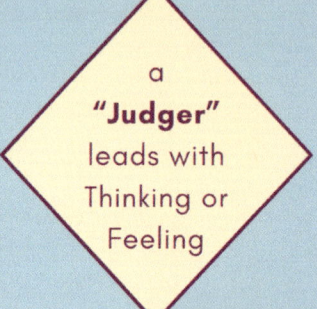

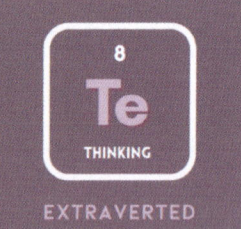

a "Judger" leads with Thinking or Feeling

a "Perceiver" leads with Intuition or Sensing

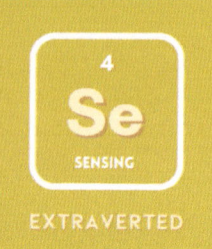

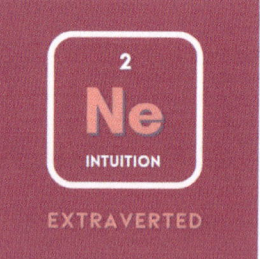

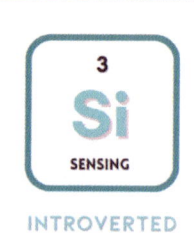

7 Ti THINKING INTROVERTED	6 Fe FEELING EXTRAVERTED
8 Te THINKING EXTRAVERTED	5 Fi FEELING INTROVERTED

1 Ni INTUITION INTROVERTED	4 Se SENSING EXTRAVERTED
2 Ne INTUITION EXTRAVERTED	3 Si SENSING INTROVERTED

"JUDGERS"
ISFP, ESFJ, ISTP, ESTJ
INFP, ENFJ, INTP, ENTJ

"PERCEIVERS"
ISFJ, ESFP, INTJ, ENTP
ISTJ, ESTP, INFJ, ENFP

Opposite of 4th letter (J/P) for Introverts
- I __ P = Judger
- E __ P = Perceiver
- I __ J = Perceiver
- E __ J = Judger

63

HALF-DUALITY

OUTERQUADRA SYMMETRIC

PERCEIVER (INFJ) — DIFF | DIFF | SAME | DIFF — (ESFP)
JUDGER — DIFF | SAME | DIFF | DIFF

Types **share HALF** of their *conscious* cognitive functions

NOTES
- Some attraction
- Some comfort
- Some repulsion
- Contrast **3** letters
- *Dominant* function is other's *Inferior*
- Can feel mysterious

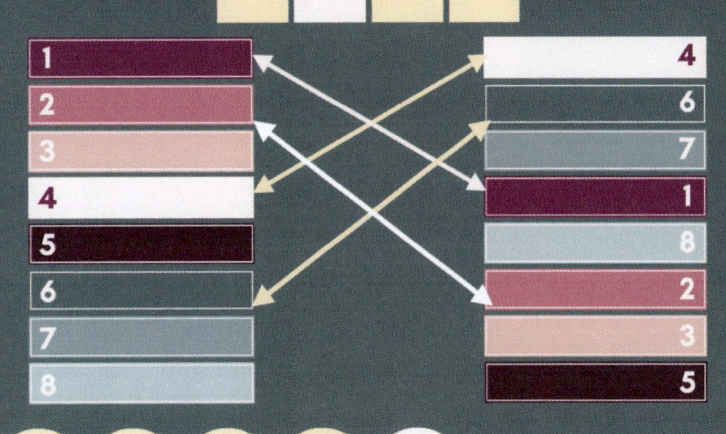

Left column: 1, 2, 3, 4, 5, 6, 7, 8
Right column: 4, 6, 7, 1, 8, 2, 3, 5

1 2 3 4 5 6 7 8 **9**

half-duality

"JUDGERS"
DIFF | SAME | DIFF | DIFF

- ISFP & ESTJ
- ISTP & ESFJ
- INFP & ENTJ
- INTP & ENFJ

"PERCEIVERS"
DIFF | DIFF | SAME | DIFF

- ISFJ & ENFP
- INTJ & ESTP
- ISTJ & ENTP
- INFJ & ESFP

KINDRED

OUTERQUADRA SYMMETRIC

PERCEIVER (INFJ) — SAME | SAME | DIFF | SAME
JUDGER (INTJ) — SAME | DIFF | SAME | SAME

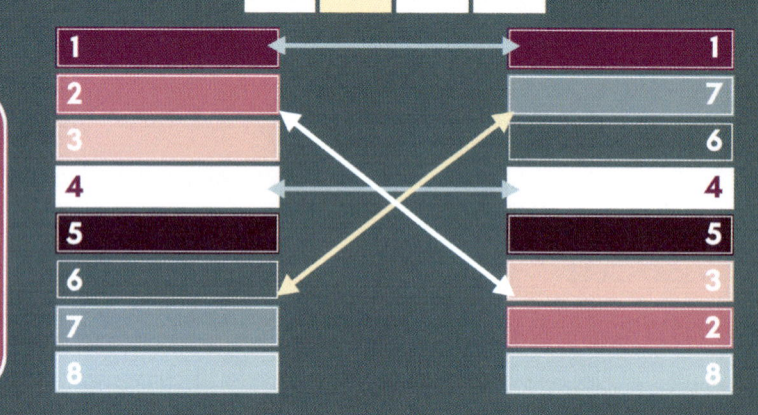

Types **share HALF** of their *conscious* cognitive functions

NOTES
- Some attraction
- Some comfort
- Some repulsion
- Contrast **1** letter
- **Same 1st function**
- Deep understanding with some surprise

Function stack pairing:
- Left: 1, 2, 3, 4, 5, 6, 7, 8
- Right: 1, 7, 6, 4, 5, 3, 2, 8

Rating: 10 / 10

"JUDGERS"
SAME | DIFF | SAME | SAME

- ENFJ & ESFJ
- ENTJ & ESTJ
- INFP & ISFP
- INTP & ISTP

kindred

"PERCEIVERS"
SAME | SAME | DIFF | SAME

- ISFJ & ISTJ
- ENFP & ENTP
- ESFP & ESTP
- INFJ & INTJ

65

MIRAGE

OUTERQUADRA SYMMETRIC

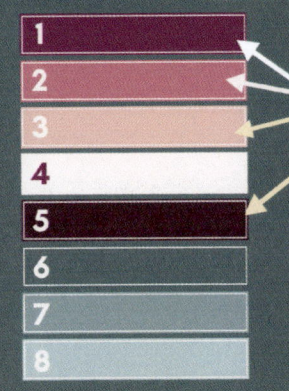

Types **share HALF** of their *conscious* cognitive functions

PERCEIVER INFJ — DIFF | SAME | DIFF | DIFF — ENTP
JUDGER — DIFF | DIFF | SAME | DIFF

NOTES
- Easy attraction
- Medium comfort
- Contrast **3** letters
- 1st & 4th functions are same type but with other attitude; mutual 2nd & 3rd

1 2 3 4 5 6 7 8 9 10 **11**

"JUDGERS"
DIFF | DIFF | SAME | DIFF

- ENFJ & ISFP
- ENTJ & ISTP
- INFP & ESFJ
- INTP & ESTJ

mirage

"PERCEIVERS"
DIFF | SAME | DIFF | DIFF

- ISTJ & ESFP
- ENFP & INTJ
- ISFJ & ESTP
- INFJ & ENTP

66

LOOK-A-LIKE

OUTERQUADRA SYMMETRIC

PERCEIVER (INFJ) SAME | DIFF | SAME | SAME (ISFJ)

JUDGER SAME | SAME | DIFF | SAME

Types share **HALF** of their *conscious* cognitive functions

NOTES
- Low attraction
- Medium comfort
- Contrast **1** letter
- Same **2nd & 3rd** functions
- *Dominant* function is other's *Trigger*

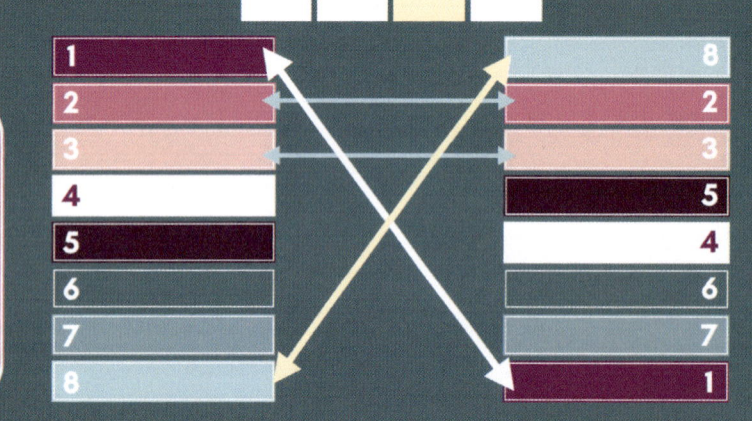

1 2 3 4 5 6 7 8 9 10 11 **12**

"JUDGERS"
SAME | SAME | DIFF | SAME

look-a-like

"PERCEIVERS"
SAME | DIFF | SAME | SAME

Judgers pairs:
- ISFP — ISTP
- ESFJ — ESTJ
- INFP — INTP
- ENFJ — ENTJ

Perceivers pairs:
- ISFJ — INFJ
- ESTP — ENTP
- ISTJ — INTJ
- ESFP — ENFP

67

SUPERVISION

OUTER QUADRA ASYMMETRIC

SUPERVISOR PERCEIVER
INFJ Supervisor — DIFF | DIFF | SAME | SAME — ESFJ Supervisee

SUPERVISOR JUDGER
ENTJ Supervisor — DIFF | SAME | DIFF | SAME — INFJ Supervisee

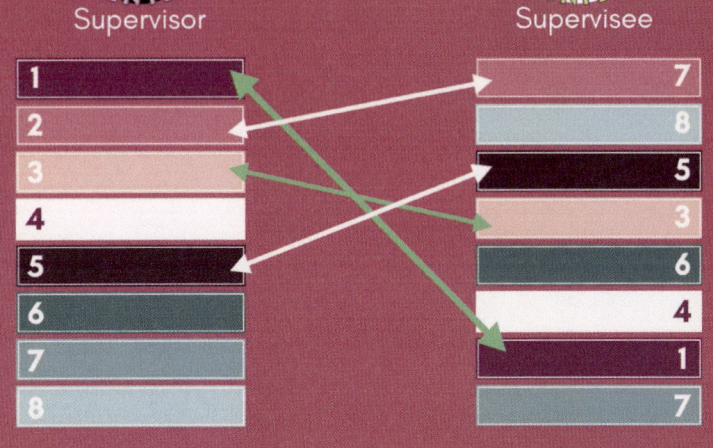

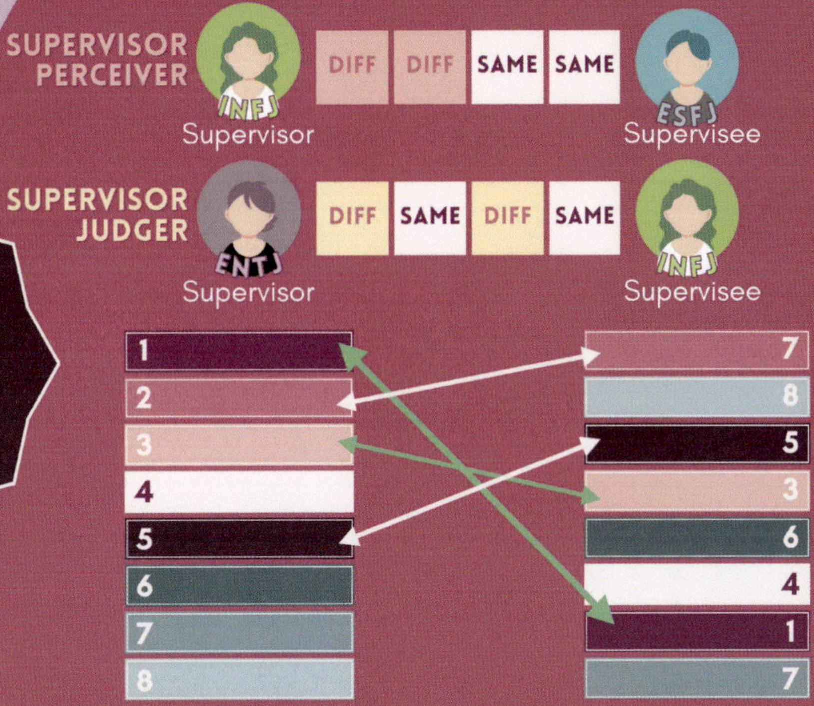

One type benefits (learns) more from this relation

Supervisor positions: 1, 2, 3, 4, 5, 6, 7, 8
Supervisee positions: 7, 8, 5, 3, 6, 4, 1, 7

NOTES
- Uneven attraction
- Comfort & repulsion
- Contrast **2** letters
- Shares HALF of conscious functions
- Supervisor's *1st* is other's *Blindspot*

1 2 3 4 5 6 7 8 9 10 11 12 **13** **14**

SUPERVISOR
ISFP | ESFJ | ISTP | ESTJ | ISFJ | ESFP | INTJ | ENTP

SUPERVISEE
ESTP | ISTJ | ESFP | ISFJ | ENFJ | INFP | ESTJ | ISTP

SUPERVISOR
INFP | ENFJ | INTP | ENTJ | ISTJ | ESTP | INFJ | ENFP

SUPERVISEE
ENTP | INTJ | ENFP | INFJ | ENTJ | INTP | ESFJ | ISFP

68

OUTERQUADRA ASYMMETRIC SOCIAL BENEFIT

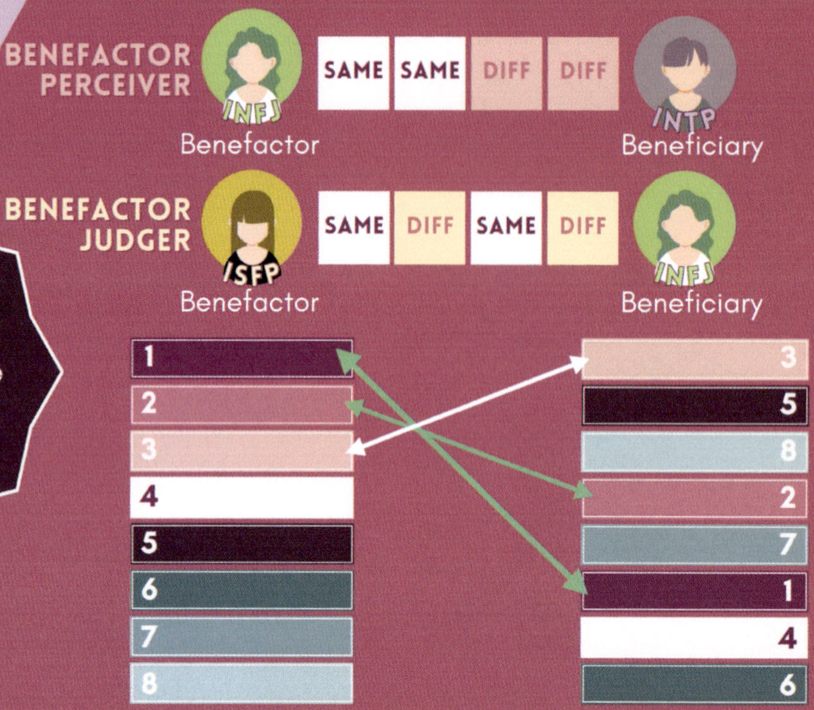

BENEFACTOR PERCEIVER
Benefactor (INFJ) — SAME | SAME | DIFF | DIFF — Beneficiary (INTP)

BENEFACTOR JUDGER
Benefactor (ISFP) — SAME | DIFF | SAME | DIFF — Beneficiary (INFJ)

One type benefits (learns) more from this relation

Benefactor functions: 1, 2, 3, 4, 5, 6, 7, 8
Beneficiary functions: 3, 5, 8, 2, 7, 1, 4, 6

NOTES
- Uneven attraction
- Easy compatibility
- Contrast **2** letters
- Shares HALF of conscious functions
- Benefactor's *1st* is other's *Critic* func.

1 2 3 4 5 6 7 8 9 10 11 12 13 14 **15** 16

BENEFACTOR
| ISFP | ESFJ | ISTP | ESTJ | ISFJ | ESFP | INTJ | ENTP |
| INFJ | ENFP | INTJ | ENTP | ISTP | ESTJ | INFP | ENFS |

BENEFICIARY

BENEFACTOR
| INFP | ENFJ | INTP | ENTJ | ISTJ | ESTP | INFJ | ENFP |
| ISFJ | ESFP | ISTJ | ESTP | ISFP | ESFJ | INTP | ENTJ |

BENEFICIARY

SECTION EIGHT

16 TYPES IN GRIP STRESS

Triggers, forms, solutions, & benefits

Grip stress occurs as a result of *excessive, unmanaged stress*. To be **"in a grip"** results in a loss of self-control and a lower general level of consciousness.

GRIPS FOR EACH TYPE

1. **Ni-Grip:** ESFP + ESTP
2. **Ne-Grip:** ISTJ + ISFJ
3. **Si-Grip:** ENFP + ENTP
4. **Se-Grip:** INTJ + INFJ
5. **Fi-Grip:** ESTJ + ENTJ
6. **Fe-Grip:** ISTP + INTP
7. **Ti-Grip:** ESFJ + ENFJ
8. **Te-Grip:** ISFP + INFP

THE ISFJ
GRIP STRESS

TRIGGERS
Circumstances that onset an Ne-Grip:
- Resisting to accept reality as it is
- Overdoing tasks
- Too much unknown while wanting a sense of control

NE-GRIP FORMS
Under stress, you can expect the ISFJ to:
- Lose control over facts & details
- Catatrophize creatively
- Be impulsive

BALANCE
Pathways back to equilibrium through:
- Firm boundaries with others
- Hitting rock bottom
- Getting help with overwhelming details

POSITIVE BENEFITS
Luckily, the ISFJ will gain experience with:
- New perspectives
- Clarity of values
- Becoming more flexible in relationships

THE ESFJ GRIP STRESS

TRIGGERS
Circumstances that onset an Ti-Grip:
- Conflict in personal relationships
- Social pressures to conform
- Feeling a lack of trust

BALANCE
Pathways back to equilibrium through:
- Starting a new, inspiring project
- Self-reflection in solitude
- Respects others' need for space

TI-GRIP FORMS
Under stress, you can expect the ESFJ to:
- Seek truth compulsively
- Overly criticize
- Overthink unnecessarily

POSITIVE BENEFITS
Luckily, the ESFJ will gain experience with:
- Reasonable reactions
- Confidence in own logical analysis
- Less need for people-pleasing

THE ISTJ
GRIP STRESS

TRIGGERS
Circumstances that onset an Ne-Grip:
- Resisting to accept reality as it is
- Overdoing tasks
- Too much unknown while wanting a sense of control

NE-GRIP FORMS
Under stress, you can expect the ISTJ to:
- Lose control over facts & details
- Catatrophize creatively
- Be impulsive

BALANCE
Pathways back to equilibrium through:
- Firm boundaries with others
- Hitting rock bottom
- Getting help with overwhelming details

POSITIVE BENEFITS
Luckily, the ISTJ will gain experience with:
- New perspectives
- Clarity of values
- Becoming more flexible in relationships

THE ESTJ
GRIP STRESS

TRIGGERS
Circumstances that onset an Fi-Grip:
- Others' freely expressed emotions
- Violation of one own's core values
- Guilt for their coldness

FI-GRIP FORMS
Under stress, you can expect the ESTJ to:
- Avoid emotions
- Have emotional outbursts
- Feel vulnerable with sensitivity

BALANCE
Pathways back to equilibrium through:
- Deeply experiencing their own feelings
- Talking honestly to a trusted confidant
- Faithful support from others

POSITIVE BENEFITS
Luckily, the ESTJ will gain experience with:
- Accept irrationality
- Prioritize important relationships
- Recognize their need for rest

THE ISFP GRIP STRESS

TRIGGERS
Circumstances that onset an Te-Grip:
- Disrespect of personal values
- Excessive criticism or negativity
- Fear of loss or disconnection

TE-GRIP FORMS
Under stress, you can expect the ISFP to:
- Act impulsively
- Harshly judge incompetence
- Aggressively criticize

BALANCE
Pathways back to equilibrium through:
- Engaging mindfully in enjoyable hobbies
- Emotional validation
- Allowing enough time to move on naturally alone

POSITIVE BENEFITS
Luckily, the ISFP will gain experience with:
- Balanced idealism
- Self-confidence of competency
- Accepting needs for power

THE ESFP
GRIP STRESS

TRIGGERS
Circumstances that onset an Ni-Grip:
- Lack of options or opportunities
- Rigid structures without freedom
- Over-obsession with the future

NI-GRIP FORMS
Under stress, you can expect the ESFP to:
- Unrealistically envision the future
- Lack clarity & feel confused
- Misinterpret

BALANCE
Pathways back to equilibrium through:
- Getting help to manage priorities
- Strategizing back-up plans in case
- Reassurance from others

POSITIVE BENEFITS
Luckily, the ESFP will gain experience with:
- Openness to good commitments
- More self-control
- Tapping into one own's intuition

76

THE ISTP
GRIP STRESS

TRIGGERS
Circumstances that onset an Fe-Grip:
- Expressed emotions that feel too strong
- Lack of fulfilling introverted needs
- Rejection of personal values

FE-GRIP FORMS
Under stress, you can expect the ISTP to:
- Feel vulnerable in relationships
- Be more sensitive emotionally
- Overdo logic

BALANCE
Pathways back to equilibrium through:
- Less obligations
- Time alone without intrusion for thinking
- Problem-solving with fun, easier challenges

POSITIVE BENEFITS
Luckily, the ISTP will gain experience with:
- Expressing deeper innermost feelings
- Accepting human irrationality
- Vulnerability

THE ESTP
GRIP STRESS

TRIGGERS
Circumstances that onset an Ni-Grip:
- Lack of options or opportunities
- Rigid structures without freedom
- Over-obsession with the future

NI-GRIP FORMS
Under stress, you can expect the ESTP to:
- Unrealistically envision the future
- Lack clarity & feel confused
- Misinterpret

BALANCE
Pathways back to equilibrium through:
- Getting help to manage priorities
- Strategizing back-up plans in case
- Reassurance from others

POSITIVE BENEFITS
Luckily, the ESTP will gain experience with:
- Openness to good commitments
- More self-control
- Tapping into one own's intuition

78

THE INFP GRIP STRESS

TRIGGERS
Circumstances that onset an Te-Grip:
- Disrespect of personal values
- Excessive criticism or negativity
- Fear of loss or disconnection

TE-GRIP FORMS
Under stress, you can expect the INFP to:
- Act impulsively
- Harshly judge incompetence
- Aggressively criticize

BALANCE
Pathways back to equilibrium through:
- Engaging mindfully in enjoyable hobbies
- Emotional validation
- Allowing enough time to move on naturally alone

POSITIVE BENEFITS
Luckily, the INFP will gain experience with:
- Balanced idealism
- Self-confidence of competency
- Accepting needs for power

THE ENFP GRIP STRESS

TRIGGERS
Circumstances that onset an Si-Grip:
- Over-tiredness or feeling exhausted
- Violation of personal values
- Focusing on too many facts

SI-GRIP FORMS
Under stress, you can expect the ENFP to:
- Overthink obsessively
- Sadly shutdown or withdraw
- Focus on their physique

BALANCE
Pathways back to equilibrium through:
- Meditation & quiet reflection
- Authentic support from others
- Addressing any physical needs

POSITIVE BENEFITS
Luckily, the ENFP will gain experience with:
- Appreciating facts & details more
- Shift in perspective
- Better planning & life structuring

THE INFJ
GRIP STRESS

TRIGGERS
Circumstances that onset an Se-Grip:
- Too much energy outwards without recharging time
- Excessive details
- Unexpected surprises

SE-GRIP FORMS
Under stress, you can expect the INFJ to:
- Aggressively react
- Hyperfocus on superficial details
- Impulsively overindulge

BALANCE
Pathways back to equilibrium through:
- Disregarding external influences
- Reflective time alone
- Less obligations in one's schedule for more free time

POSITIVE BENEFITS
Luckily, the INFJ will gain experience with:
- Level-headed pursuit of goals
- Better adaptability
- More moderate indulgence

THE ENFJ
GRIP STRESS

TRIGGERS
Circumstances that onset an Ti-Grip:
- Conflict in personal relationships
- Social pressures to conform
- Feeling a lack of trust

TI-GRIP FORMS
Under stress, you can expect the ENFJ to:
- Seek truth compulsively
- Overly criticize
- Overthink unnecessarily

BALANCE
Pathways back to equilibrium through:
- Starting a new, inspiring project
- Self-reflection in solitude
- Respects others' need for space

POSITIVE BENEFITS
Luckily, the ENFJ will gain experience with:
- Reasonable reactions
- Confidence in own logical analysis
- Less need for people-pleasing

THE INTP GRIP STRESS

TRIGGERS
Circumstances that onset an Fe-Grip:
- Expressed emotions that feel too strong
- Lack of fulfilling introverted needs
- Rejection of personal values

FE-GRIP FORMS
Under stress, you can expect the INTP to:
- Feel vulnerable in relationships
- Be more sensitive emotionally
- Overdo logic

BALANCE
Pathways back to equilibrium through:
- Less obligations
- Time alone without intrusion for thinking
- Problem-solving with fun, easier challenges

POSITIVE BENEFITS
Luckily, the INTP will gain experience with:
- Expressing deeper innermost feelings
- Accepting human irrationality
- Vulnerability

THE ENTP GRIP STRESS

TRIGGERS
Circumstances that onset an Si-Grip:
- Over-tiredness or feeling exhausted
- Violation of personal values
- Focusing on too many facts

SI-GRIP FORMS
Under stress, you can expect the ENTP to:
- Overthink obsessively
- Sadly shutdown or withdraw
- Focus on their physique

BALANCE
Pathways back to equilibrium through:
- Meditation & quiet reflection
- Authentic support from others
- Addressing any physical needs

POSITIVE BENEFITS
Luckily, the ENTP will gain experience with:
- Appreciating facts & details more
- Shift in perspective
- Better planning & life structuring

THE INTJ GRIP STRESS

TRIGGERS
Circumstances that onset an Se-Grip:
- Too much energy outwards without recharging time
- Excessive details
- Unexpected surprises

SE-GRIP FORMS
Under stress, you can expect the INTJ to:
- Aggressively react
- Hyperfocus on superficial details
- Impulsively overindulge

BALANCE
Pathways back to equilibrium through:
- Disregarding external influences
- Reflective time alone
- Less obligations in one's schedule for more free time

POSITIVE BENEFITS
Luckily, the INTJ will gain experience with:
- Level-headed pursuit of goals
- Better adaptability
- More moderate indulgence

THE ENTJ
GRIP STRESS

TRIGGERS
Circumstances that onset an Fi-Grip:
- Others' freely expressed emotions
- Violation of one own's core values
- Guilt for their coldness

FI-GRIP FORMS
Under stress, you can expect the ENTJ to:
- Avoid emotions
- Have emotional outbursts
- Feel vulnerable with sensitivity

BALANCE
Pathways back to equilibrium through:
- Deeply experiencing their own feelings
- Talking honestly to a trusted confidant
- Faithful support from others

POSITIVE BENEFITS
Luckily, the ENTJ will gain experience with:
- Accept irrationality
- Prioritize important relationships
- Recognize their need for rest

A thankful conclusion

You've reached the end of my **Ultimate 16 Personalities Visual Guide** & I hope you enjoyed it! Now you have forever have a resource to reference & learn from.

I outlined it in a way that builds off of the basics to appreciate all of the depth this personality framework offers. Of course, there is *so much more* that could be explored in each focus. I will continue to create more content, so if you liked this **MBTI Cheat Sheet**, do stick around. Check my site **Quest In** from time to time to read articles, enjoy podcasts, and access new products or services I offer!

As I write this, I am currently 6 months pregnant with my second baby while my son is a wild toddler. The last few years have been *CRAZY* and full of growth, but there was a lot of just trying to make it through in survival mode...

When my son was a newborn, I started my website as an outlet for my mind after spending the entire day in my senses. I wanted to create something useful and beautiful to share with others *from my heart*. It has been a truly fulfilling project to build up and openly publish. I attempt to infuse each piece I make with love!

Thank you for being a part of this meaningful connection via the internet with me. Wherever you may be in the world, I am wishing you well. Blessings from California!

Copyright ©2024 by Quest In. All Rights Reserved.

TAKE MY FREE QUICK MBTI QUIZ
https://thequestinpodcast.com/quick-mbti-personality-test/

TAKE THE WHAT'S YOUR IDEAL TYPE QUIZ
https://thequestinpodcast.com/ideal-type-quiz/

CHECK OUT MY WEBSITE SHOP
https://thequestinpodcast.com/sale/

CONTACT@THEQUESTINPODCAST.COM

Printed in Great Britain
by Amazon